CW01495012

Manfred Zainzinger, Sabine Knoll

BOWTECH®

The Original Bowen Technique

Healing the body gently
Moves that promote health and wellbeing

Releasing pain and tension
aiding the healing process

Contents

What is Bowtech?

Bowtech, the original Bowen technique is a gentle, holistic method of treatment for the body, working on muscles, tendons and peripheral nerves. A few moves with very little pressure rebalance the body and restore its self-healing power. Bowtech only generates impulses; the rebalancing of the body takes place by itself.

©CreativeCollection

Moves to increase your self-healing power

We all have the "blueprint" for the healthy condition of our body, a matrix of health. Due to our way of life, which drifts away from our origins, body, soul and mind are put under pressure, leaving us feeling stressed. The body forgets about its original state of health and completeness. This can lead to a feeling of illness. Bowtech reminds the body, in a very gentle way, of its matrix of health. A few gentle impulses and moves can rebalance the body- it can revoke a healthy condition. In other words, our bio computer is updated!

Less is more

This concept of health is the basis of the original Australian Bowen technique. Developed in the middle of the 20th century, it has become a technique for the new age.

No great manipulations, because less is more. Bowtech sends homeopathic impulses. As in homeopathy as well, high potencies – the preparations with the lowest material part of the healing substance – are the most effective. The information, the healing vibrations, are nevertheless felt and therefore highly effective from the energy point of view.

Bowtech makes the body more conscious of itself and more sensitive. Thanks to their better general balance after a treatment, people often notice that they feel stronger within, able to make clearer decisions and are more optimistic and confident, too.

The Bowen technique is performed by hand, on the body or on light clothing. A practitioner performs single rolling moves, then leaves the patient alone in order to give the body a chance to integrate, "store" and process the impulses. The body as an instrument is again "tuned up". The therapist returns to perform the next moves, followed by a short break again. The technique does not seem spectacular. The treatment is usually completed after about 30 minutes, and the next session is usually one week later – in most cases between 5 to 10 days. A few days later, the symptoms may have already disappeared,

Often only a few Bowtech moves are needed to provide lasting relief of problems.

sometimes completely, and the cause of the disorder is cleared after 2 or 3 treatments. Ten or more sessions may be needed, depending on the gravity of the illness, or in case of chronic conditions.

What effect actually does this "miracle technique" produce by stimulating the energy flow within the body thereby allowing it to adjust itself, supporting all other treatment?

What Bowtech triggers off in the body

Bowtech rebalances the body

In the Far East the energetic concept is a balance between Yin and Yang, the polarities. Everything flows and is a part of the whole. If one element is imbalanced, the whole balance is disturbed. Gentle impulses can support the body to bring it back into equilibrium. The balance between the left and the right half of the body plays an important role.

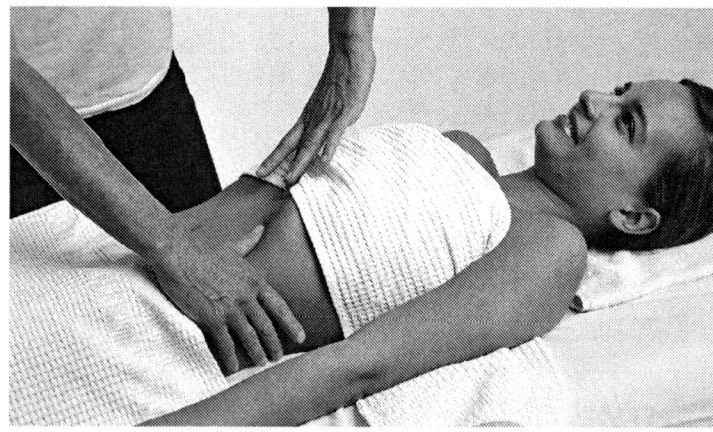

The body reacts instantly to an applied move – unlike massage, where points are massaged longer.

Bowtech relaxes the body

Only a few moves help the body to reach a level of deep relaxation. In this state everything is easy. The autonomic nervous system calms down, the body can work in peace and find its equilibrium. Healing is possible. Many people fall asleep during the treatment. This can even be a sign of relief, especially for "thinking" types of people for whom it is difficult to let go.

Bowtech stimulates the self-healing power

Starting from the brain, information is transferred to the body. When moves are applied to specific points, the body becomes aware of the area needing attention. This is followed by a flow of energy and nerve impulses. Because of the interaction of the nerves and other control points within the body, effects can occur in other parts of the body as well.

The body reacts instantly to an applied move – unlike massage, where points are massaged longer.

Bowtech releases the energy flow

In Far-Eastern medicine, the energy conductors of the body are called "meridians". As well as the nerves, which are used in Western medicine as an explanation for the effect, the meridians and their increased energy flow can also support healing processes. More vitality is noticeable through the energy flow.

Bowtech stimulates the circulation and the lymphatic flow

Not only energy circulates in our body but also blood and lymph. The latter is responsible for detoxification. If the lymph flow is blocked, the body cannot completely clear the wasteproducts from the tissue. Moreover, oedema – fluid accumulation in the tissue can occur.

Bowtech gently stimulates the circulation as well as the lymph flow, which again activates the expulsion of toxins.

Bowtech also has a preventive effect. It strengthens the immune system, activates the circulation as well as the lymphatic and nervous systems and stimulates the body functions. Regular treatment helps the body to keep its balance on all levels, so that illness can not develop.

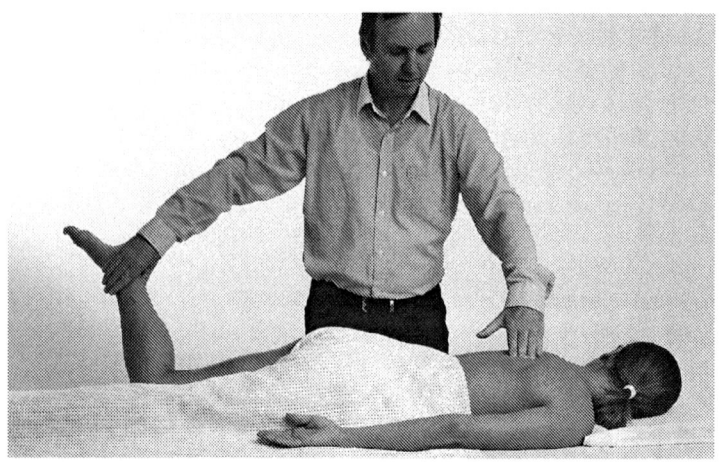

As well as the moves and their sequences it is important that the therapist gives the body time to interpret these signals.

Bowtech stimulates the intake of nutrients and oxygen

In this way nutrients can be more easily transported from the stomach and digestive system into the cells. It is of course very important in this context to consciously follow a healthy diet with enough nutrients.

> *The major part of healing occurs after the Bowen treatment. The body heals itself, it needs time for this and the best possible conditions in its surroundings, which will support it.*

Bowtech considerably improves the intake of oxygen to the lungs, a positive effect when there is difficulty in breathing. Sufficient exercise lets the body breathe more deeply thus providing more oxygen, an important basis of our health.

Bowtech relaxes muscles and tendons

Occasionally, muscles become tense because of stress and try to adopt a protective position in order to avoid pain and to make parts of the body immobile. Bowtech gently loosens up the muscles without causing pain.

Bowtech improves the mobility of the fascia

Fascia is the membrane which shapes the muscle tissue. The Bowtech therapy dissolves adhesions. Also scarred tissue becomes softer without putting undue pressure on the fascia.

The Bowtech effect on emotions

Without being one of its targets, Bowtech can trigger emotions because the body never forgets. Past traumas settle in the body's memory and act as crystallization points on different levels of the body. Bowtech sometimes dissolves such crystallized emotions. It can make relieving tears flow and healing may also occur on the emotional level.

What Bowtech is not

It is more difficult to answer the question what Bowtech exactly is than what the technique is not. Since it cannot be compared to anything else, it however reminds one of several other methods. Although Bowtech, for instance, triggers off the energy flow and deals not only with the body, but also the energy system, the method cannot be explicitly understood as energy work, because the therapists do not make themselves a channel for energy transference. Even if Bowtech always includes a holistic comprehension of body, soul and mind, this technique is neither a pure body method, nor a pure spiritual one.

Pain is a warning sign that something is out of balance in the body. To maintain a healthy body you need to have a balanced diet, exercise and relaxation.

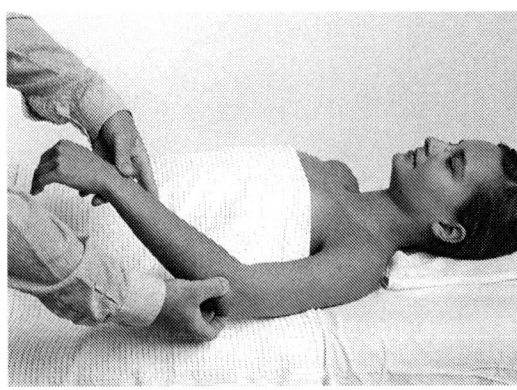

This hands on therapy stimulates emotional releases and relaxation promoting a return to a feeling of well-being.

Holistic health is a state of harmony of body, mind and spirit. It is defined by a clear and balanced person who is full of energy. People, who are healthy in body, mind and spirit, feel happy and contented.

Bowtech is not a massage

Although the technique deals with muscles and the connective tissue, gentle touch is all that is needed. There is no deep and some- times painful massage in Bowtech. Muscles are not kneaded until they are soft, they simply loosen on their own as the moves are applied.

Bowtech is not acupressure

Some points which Bowtech moves touch, are identical with acu- pressure points, others not. Bowtech does not stimulate certain points on the meridians. Nevertheless it also has an effect on the meridian system.

Bowtech is not a trigger-point therapy

There are many parallels but this therapy has not directly influenced Bowtech. While trigger-points are mostly situated in the middle of the muscle being pressed to release tension, Bowtech treats the area where two muscles or muscle groups overlap, at the muscular inser- tion or via nerves and tendons as well.

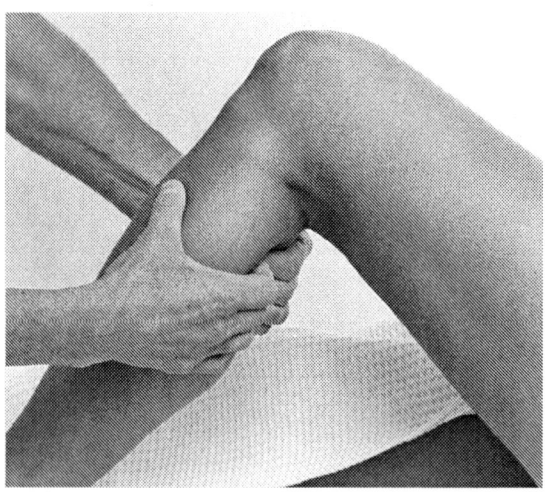

The KISS-rule is also valuable for Bowtech: keep it short and simple – less is more!

Bowtech is not a lymphatic drainage

The lymph flow is stimulated by Bowtech, however there are no specific strokes and stimuli of the lymph flow as in a lymphatic drainage.

Bowtech is not a therapy of muscular sheath relief

Although the Bowtech moves act on the fascia, the muscular sheath, there is no specific and deep treatment of the fascia as with Rolfing. The moves there are made with more pressure, which can even be painful. This is not true for Bowtech.

Bowen moves are gentle and can also be performed through clothing.

Bowtech is not a chiropractic therapy

Even if dislocated joints and vertebrae can reset themselves by the work on muscles and tendons, Bowtech neither acts on the skeleton nor on the bony tissue. There are no strong jerky thrusts as in chiropractic.

Bowtech is not physiotherapy

Although sometimes simple exercises will be recommended to support treatment, they do not aim at body training. Moving the body, as in walking, is helpful for the detoxification, but strenuous

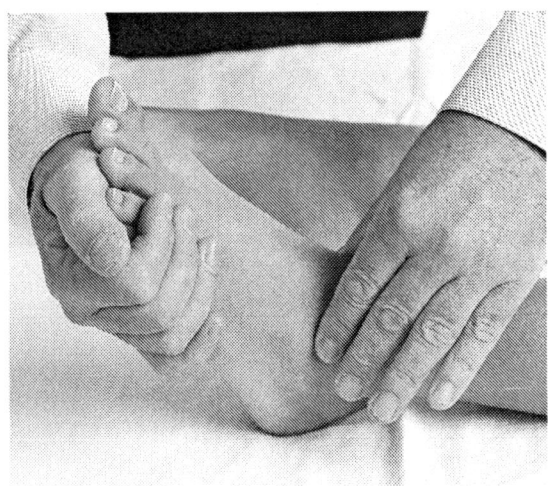

Bowen is especially effective in sport injuries.

exercise on the day of treatment and some days later may interfere with a beneficial outcome.

Bowtech works without aid
No oil or vibration, electricity, magnetism or implements are used. Treatment happens exclusively with the hands.

Bowtech is not body psychotherapy
Although the moves can trigger off emotions, it is not the aim when using this method. Emotions can drain away with the energies, which are dissolved in the body. Often people report a feeling of well-being and clarity after treatment.

Sportsmen use Bowen to improve their performance.

Bowtech is not energy work

Similar to Reiki, Polarity and other methods, work is carried out with the hands, which stimulates the body and energy system, increasing energy flow, however it does not consciously transfer energy to the body.

Although Bowtech is a relatively new modality, it has become widespread internationally.

Bowtech is not a religion

In order to experience the Bowtech effect, you need neither be religious nor part of any other doctrine. Being open to treatment and healing, however supports the process as with any other method and healing work.

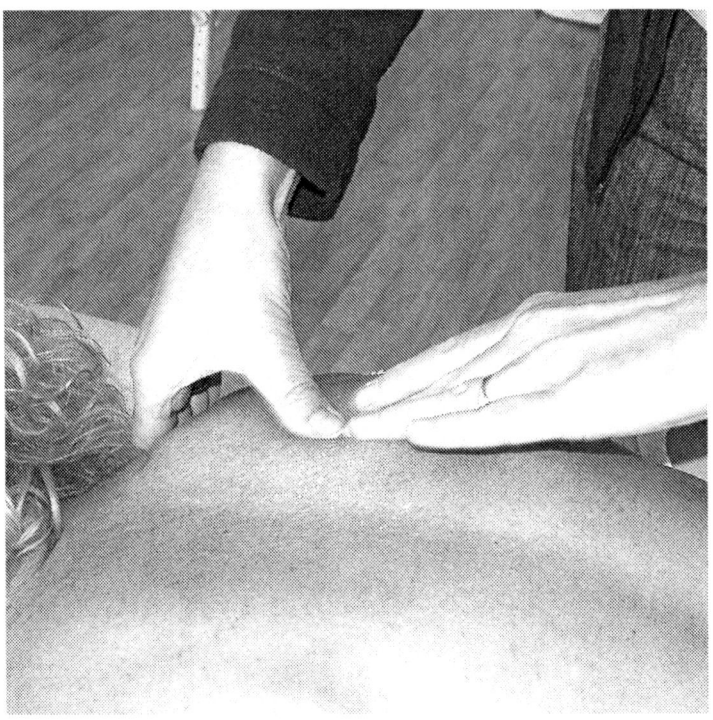

Bowtech helps the body to heal itself.

The development of Bowtech

It began in Australia: the birthplace of Tom Ambrose Bowen, the man whose name still lives on through Bowtech. He was a silent and religious man; little is reported about his life. Only after his death the technique, which was put in a teachable format by his student Oswald Rentsch, spread worldwide.

©CreativeCollection

Tom Bowen, the man behind Bowtech

Tom Bowen came from a humble background. His parents, emigrants from Great Britain, settled down in Melbourne in the south-east of Australia, where Tom Ambrose Bowen was born in April 1916. They were very religious people and active in the Salvation Army. In the early 1940's the Bowen family moved to Geelong in the federal state of Victoria, where Tom, like his father, worked in the local cement works, after he had left compulsory school. He also trained young people in the sports club of the Salvation Army in his spare

Tom Ambrose Bowen (1916-1982), founder of the Bowen technique.

time. Even at that time he was interested in the work of healing, although his family could not afford for him to attend medical university. In the local soccer club, Tom Bowen loved to watch over the masseurs' shoulders and over time he began treating injured sportsmen himself.

A gift from God

Although Tom Bowen never received any training in body therapy or other methods of treatment, he knew by intuition what the body needed to rebalance and regenerate itself. He called this his "gift from God", the ability to sense which move to make in order to stimulate and

Although modest and reserved, Tom Bowen quickly made a name for himself in Australia.

support the body's self healing power. He called himself an osteopath a common practice at that time for practitioners, who were working on the human body, however he was never admitted to the association for osteopaths. His work differed significantly from the classic osteopathy, so Tom Bowen was seen as more the creator of a new form of manual therapy.

In this house Bowen opened his first practice.

Injured players from the soccer team, who had been treated by Tom Bowen, were able to continue playing after only a few moves. It is said that in the cement plant as well he provided first aid with his soft technique to injured workers, leading to much faster recovery.

Tom Bowen's treatment was mostly not spectacular, but characterized by his deep love for the people who came to him. More and more patients were queuing to see him when he returned home from work. Tom Bowen treated them in friends' houses for half the night.

His wife Jessie, a severe asthmatic herself, could breathe more freely thanks to her husband's method of treatment. Gradually Tom Bowen's "gift from God" became a fulltime job. Even animals showed significant improvement after his treatment and so the animal-loving man was always ready to help injured dogs, cats, cows, pigs and horses.

His own practice

Since the large number of people coming to Tom Bowen could no longer be dealt with on top of his work anymore, he founded his own practice in Geelong in the late 1950's. The clinic was situated in an old house in an area where the majority of doctors in Geelong also practised. Tom Bowen turned his house into a cosy treatment centre. The waiting room was full of craftwork and needlework from his handicapped patients. Often 15 people or more waited there for treatment. Tom Bowen worked six hours a day in his clinic and devoted himself to house calls for bedridden people in the evenings. Usually 50 to 60 people came for treatment every day.

Every second Saturday his appointment book was reserved for handicapped people, especially physically handicapped such as spastics, who Tom Bowen treated for free and who regained higher mobility thanks to him. His door was also wide open for asthma patients and pregnant women. Furthermore he often treated prisoners in the Geelong prison on Sundays.

As an assistant at Tom Bowen's side was the woman who, together with her husband, had already put her house at his disposal as the first treatment room – Rene Horwood. She was the good spirit of his surgery, always spreading an ambience of joy and well-being and supporting Tom in his work from the bottom of her heart.

The success of the Bowen technique became even more widespread: In 1975 Tom Bowen was already treating over 13,000 clients a year.

Word of his success with healing travelled widely. According to a 27 week study by the government of the federal state of Victoria, Tom Bowen was one of the most sought-after and successful therapists of the country in 1975, treating over 13,000 clients every year. A surprisingly high number, if one considers that most of the clients only received two or three treatment sessions at a maximum of once a week. His success rate of healing was 88 %. In time Bowen's

His assistant Rene Horwood supported and stood loyally by Tom Bowen for many years.

technique became one of the world's most successful holistic treatment methods.

In his surgery Tom Bowen worked in two rooms concurrently. After having done some moves he left the room to allow the body to respond and to let the moves take effect, and then he went into the next room, where he began treatment as well. After some minutes he went back into the first room and so on. At first Tom Bowen's patients lay on normal beds, which created a confidential and relaxing atmosphere and also assisted in the success of treatment. Several years later the first massage table found its way into the practice.

Tom Bowen knew intuitively where the cause of the problem was.

Tom Bowen was a man of few words during his work. Usually he talked to his clients only for a very short time in order to give them hints, recipes and exercises for home use to assist the treatment. He communicated mostly with the people who accompanied or assisted him or who studied with him by hand signs. This was also probably because Tom Bowen became more and more hard of hearing as he got older and finally wore a hearing aid. However his fingers became more sensitive, like keen sensors, by which he was able to detect tension and energy blockages in the body's nervous and muscular system.

While he was helping the people he treated, Tom Bowen often forgot about himself. As a result of his diabetes he finally lost one leg and for a year could only move with the help of an artificial limb. Shortly before his death, his second leg also had to be amputated, which didn't deter him from continuing to provide treatment. From then on he moved in a wheelchair between the treatment tables through his surgery. Until his death Tom Bowen never stopped supporting other people through their illnesses.

The Rentschs come to Tom Bowen

At a health congress in Adelaide, South-Australia, in 1974 Tom Bowen met the couple Oswald and Elaine Rentsch. Oswald « Ossie » Rentsch was a farmer at that time and had started training for massage and osteopathy in order to be able to help his wife Elaine.

Tom Bowen searched for a long time for the right therapists to pass on his technique.

Elaine had fallen out of a moving car when she was a four year old child and had injured her cervical and thoracic spine badly, which caused continuous pain. The doctors, who were treating her, predicted that she would need a wheelchair by the age of 30. All therapies had proved ineffective and Elaine nearly gave up: "When Ossie touched me, I only cried with pain".

When Tom Bowen and the Rentsch couple were introduced to each other by a friend, a magic moment happened. "I said to Tom Bowen, without knowing him or having ever heard of him: "Mr. Bowen, I would like to learn from you". And Ossie remembers Tom Bowen's answer at that fateful meeting: "Okay, I will teach you." The invitation to come to his surgery the following Wednesday finally led to two and a half years of learning, observing and recording.

"I expect to pass through this world but once,
any good thing therefore that I do,
or any kindness that I can show
to any fellow-creature, let me do it now.
Let me not defer or neglect it,
for I shall not pass this way again".

Quotation from Tom Bowen's study

"Tom urged me to accompany him, to watch his fingers and to try the moves myself as well. Doing so he corrected me again and again", Oswald Rentsch explains. And when Tom Bowen was ill himself, his most talented student became his stand in, who worked up a sweat – considering of Tom Bowen's daily work quota.

Oswald's wife Elaine came to Tom Bowen for treatment as well. "When he touched my neck for the first time, he just said: 'We will put it right, but it might take time'. He estimated half a year', Elaine remembers. "But when I drove home with Ossie, I said to him: 'Something is different'. It didn't even take half a year and my life started again. Today I play golf, tennis, badminton, squash and I even ride horses." Sometimes you can see Ossie and Elaine together on a motorbike.

Bowtech becomes independent

In 1976 Ossie and Elaine Rentsch opened their own naturopathic surgery in Hamilton, Victoria – with Tom Bowen's blessing. They were in contact with their teacher for another six years in order to continuously refine and perfect the treatment technique. Only after Tom Bowen's death in 1982, the idea to pass on the method was born. "On his deathbed I promised to carry his name and his work into the world", Oswald Rentsch says. "He said: 'Thank you, my son' ". Tom Bowen's real son devoted himself to his career as a pianist, and also his two daughters were not interested in the legacy of healing work. Nevertheless four more years passed by until Ossie and Elaine Rentsch decided to really teach the method.

info

In contrast to other manual therapies, it is the goal of the Bowen technique to enable the body to heal itself by minimal intervention.

"In Hamilton, where I practised, other therapists often came to see me and told me: 'If you don't go out and teach, all this will be lost to the world.'" But Bowtech was not a complete training, Bowtech was Tom Bowen's life. So Oswald Rentsch decided to give the technique a teachable format, calling it "Bowtech – the original Bowen technique". After having been a farmer, masseur and Bowen practitioner – he now became a teacher as well. "Over the years Tom Bowen allowed only six people to observe him at his work for longer periods. They were osteopaths, chiropractors etc. and they didn't want to teach. They thought Bowtech could not be taught and furthermore their surgeries were fully booked", Oswald Rentsch explains. So it was really up to him to keep his promise and carry Bowtech out into the world.

The first seminar took place in Perth in Western Australia in 1986, a four hour flight away from the Rentsch's home in the east. "There nobody knew me, which was good, in case I made a fool of myself", Oswald Rentsch laughs today when he remembers that time. Quite the contrary, the seminar was highly successful and word quickly spread.

The Rentsches, introduced Bowen Therapy to the world.

"The next course was in Melbourne. A man, who sold vitamin and mineral preparations, had invited and organized the course for us. His magazine had published only two lines on the Bowtech seminar, but 180 people replied to us!" Tom Bowen's work had become well known and the chance to get to know his method personally was a sensation. "Consequently we gave six seminars per year in Melbourne and further courses in other Australian towns, each lasting four to five days."

The technique spreads all over the world

Four years later the huge success of the seminars led Ossie and Elaine Rentsch to fully concentrate on teaching and so gave up their practice.

In 1999 the organizer of the seminars moved to America and started to treat people there. This was so successful that many of them wanted to learn Bowtech themselves. This led to the first seminars in the United States of America.

"We never decided to go to 25 countries to teach Bowtech, as we are now doing. This has developed on its own because people from very

In order to preserve the technique in its original form, the Rentsches founded the Bowen Therapy Academy of Australia in 1987 and named the therapy Bowtech – the original Bowen technique.

There are now branches of the Bowtech Academy in the USA, UK, Germany, Austria, Switzerland and many other countries.

different countries have learnt from us and carried the technique further", Oswald Rentsch explains.

Meanwhile Bowtech is known in Australia and New Zealand, North America, Great Britain, South Africa and large parts of Europe. Russia, Japan and Brazil have also shown interest. The duration of the seminars has grown from four days at first to 14 days now and since 1994 not only thousands of practising therapists have been trained, but also more than 70 instructors who teach the technique and pass on Bowtech in its original form. A worldwide snowball process has started.

"Does it hurt? – No?
Is it a problem? – No?
So don't worry about it."

Tom Bowen's advice for people coming to him

Also scientifically recognized

The provisional appraisal of 2004 has shown that already more than 17,000 people all over the world have been trained by Ossie and Elaine Rentsch and their network "Bowen Therapy Academy of Australia".

In Australia the technique is now recognized by traditional medicine as an effective method, even several doctors outside Australia practise Bowtech as a supportive and complementary form to traditional medicine and several scientific research projects have proved the effectiveness of the work.

Bowtech does not only influence biochemical processes in the body, but also produces a more relaxed mood and pleasant emotions, which has a positive effect on the person's whole state.

A leader in research is the American doctor and Bowtech therapist Jo Ann Whitaker from Florida, carrying out ongoing studies at her institute. She frequently recommends Bowtech training to her medical colleagues.

Jo Ann Whitaker has worked as a doctor in crisis areas such as Vietnam, Bosnia, Serbia and India, where she taught Bowtech moves to people with no medical background at all.

Bowtech is copied

The success of the Bowen technique has not only brought authorized teachers on to the scene. "Approximately 20 people have star-

The Bowen technique is taught all over the world – also in Italy - by Ossie and Elaine Rentsch.

ted their own Bowen training, some of them under a different name", says Oswald Rentsch unhappy that the technique has also spread in a modified form. Only "Bowtech – the original Bowen technique" is the registered and legally protected original method developed by Tom Bowen.

The original becomes established

"To mix Bowtech with other methods is counterproductive", believes Oswald Rentsch, who initially thought to combine massage and osteopathy with Bowtech. However, less is sometimes more. Tom Bowen knew that the body had the power of healing within itself and that too much information could easily overload it.

However, despite all attempts to copy the successful technique, in the end quality will always succeed and Oswald Rentsch puts his trust in the power of the original.

Muscles, fascia & co.

The body consists of muscles, fascia, nerves and ener-
gy pathways, which communicate with each other.
Bowen stimulates these systems to work together to
restore balance.

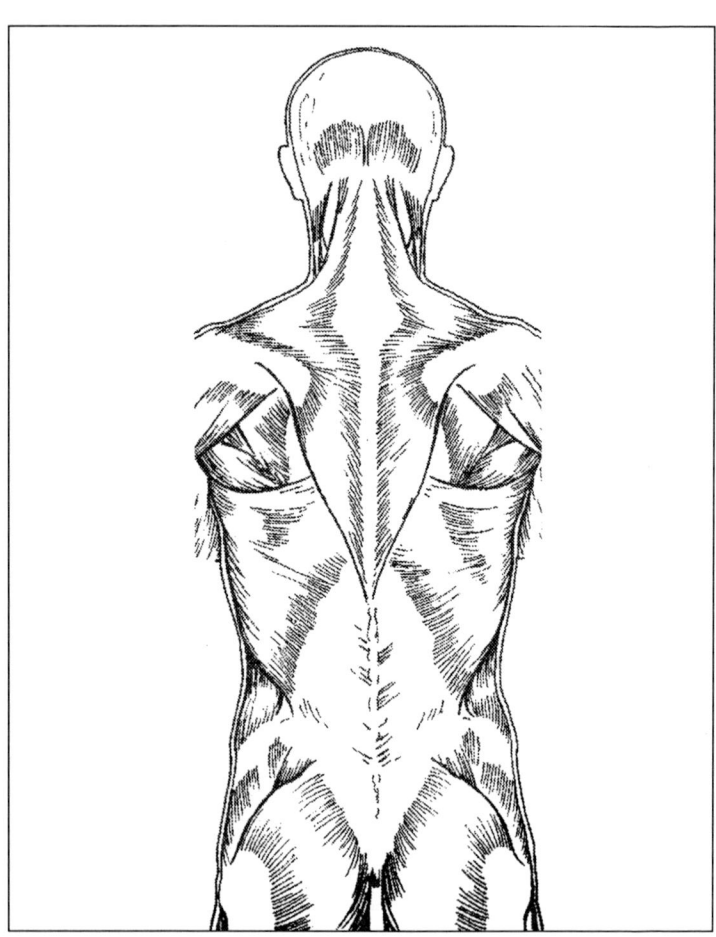

Where Bowtech starts and how the method works

There are different theories from East and West, explaining why Bowtech works. Whichever system, either the Far-East science of meridians or Western traditional medicine, every method of explanation has something to be said for it. In this chapter you will find an overview of the most important results of research on how and why the method works and where it starts. Among others, the Bowtech moves pass on self-healing impulses to the muscles and fascia – the connective tissue of the body.

The interplay of muscles

Our organism would not work without muscles. They support and move the skeleton and are involved in numerous processes inside the body - from swallowing to breathing and distributing blood.

The musculature occupies the biggest part of the body – almost 50% of normal-weight people are muscle mass – and it is the largest energy consumer of the organism. Our organs are basically responsible for the growth and supply to the musculature as well as the maintenance of the body functions.

> **info**
>
> Different from trigger point therapies or osteopathy, Bowtech stimulates only on the muscle surface, but does not directly treat deeper tissue layers.

Among the most important muscles of the body are the long extensors of the back, which hold the backbone upright and make walking on two feet possible for us. They are the neuromuscular link between sacrum and cranium. Every imbalance due to tension in this area can lead to trapped nerves and other disorders, which spread from the spine's nervous system over the whole body.

Other very essential muscles for the posture and the body functions are the hip-joint flexors, which stabilise the hip joint, the lower-leg tensors or "thigh adductor" and the trapezius muscles between the shoulder blades.

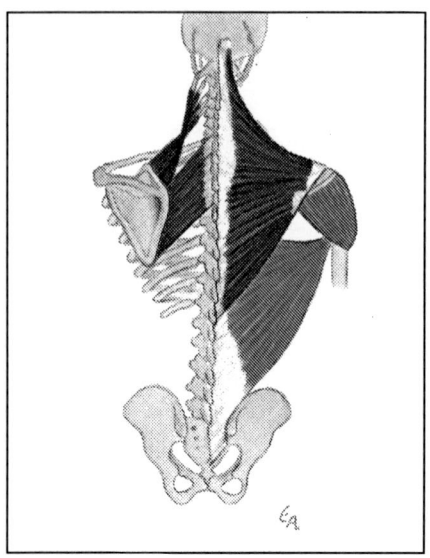

The trapezius muscles and the long extensors of the back are important muscles for the interplay of the whole body. This is a frequent area for tension in the upper body.

The correct muscle tension is decisive for our health. Muscles which are too limp are not able to support the skeleton sufficiently – this leads to bad posture, the pelvis can slip and consequently the vertebrae, which has an effect on the whole body. The musculature tries to compensate and tenses up in other areas in order to stabilise the posture.

A great deal of energy bound and lost in chronically tensioned muscles could be more useful for the organism as the power for daily tasks and to supply our activities with vitality. One task of Bowtech is to free this energy and loosen up blockages. Since a body with chronically tensioned muscles has the same effect as trying to drive a vehicle with the handbrake on, the energy is used up many times over, leading to exhaustion and becoming more prone to illnesses.

Fascia – the net of our body

If you removed everything from a human body apart from the fascia, it would still have the look and structure of a human body. The fascia – the connective tissue between and around the muscles, organs, blood vessels, nerves and bones – mainly consists of collagenous fibres and gives the body its structure. It has a protective effect like shock absorbers and also has other important functions.

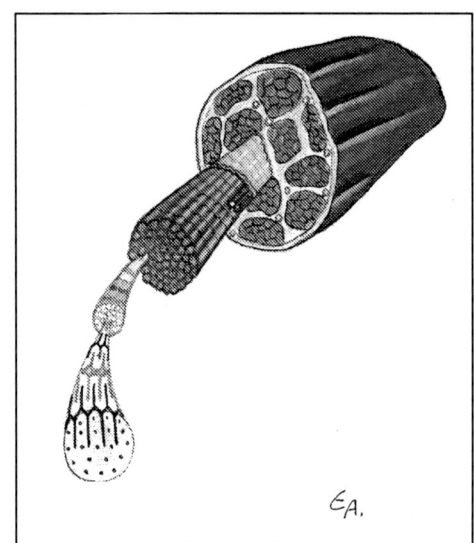

Muscles are a highly complex system with one main goal: to hold the apparatus of movement upright and move it.

Support for the body

The fascia in our body makes our muscular system work and provides the interplay of the individual muscles. It gives the muscles form, connects them to the bones and as a ligament keeps the joints sturdy but mobile. Even every single muscular fibre is wrapped in fascia.

Fascia fixes the inner organs to our skeletal structure, wraps them protectively and supplies a perfect cohesion. Together with the muscular system it supports the vertebral column and enables our erect posture. Fascia can be very solid – in the area of the ligaments – or very loose in structure – in the area of glands. Furthermore it is often very elastic, such as the uterus during pregnancy, which contracts after birth back to the original size again.

About 50% of the body weight is muscle mass. In total man has approx. 640 muscles. The largest is the flat back muscle, the smallest the stapedius muscle in the ear.

A supporting role

The fascia is the supporting structure for the nervous, vascular and lymphatic system. The nerves and vessels are interwoven with the

Even if Bowen stimulates only very gently and does not treat the skelature by itself, as in e.g. Osteopathy. This technique has an effect on the posture of the client.

fascia. Every nerve, every vessel is wrapped in fascia and the fine vibrations of the fascia are like a pump for the lymphatic flow as well as for the venous blood system, actively supporting the circulation of these fluids in the body. The micro-motions of the fascia and the tension in this area can be felt with the hands. A gift and sensitivity which Tom Bowen had in abundance from the day he was born and further developed.

An elastic protective cover

Stress and trauma from outside are a danger to the body and its vulnerable organs. The fascia is responsible for good protection of the soft parts and absorbs a great deal that could lead to injuries. It is particularly adaptable and elastic. Those who have cut up a piece of meat know the fascia as the silvery-white muscular coat around the flesh, which sometimes can hardly be cut through. The more strain a body part is exposed to, the thicker the fascia is, e.g. at the joints and in the peripheral areas of the body. It never becomes hard and stiff even when very thick.

Many euphoric reports from clients, doctors and therapists prove that Bowtech helps. There are several theories on how Bowtech works.

Shock absorbers of the body

Due to its elastic character, the fascia has an effect like shock absorbers, which absorb strain. Tension and influences from outside are absorbed in this way, so that they do not collide against organs and muscular fascia with full force. In some very strained body areas, such as the back or lumbar region, the fascia sometimes becomes gelatinous and viscous like lubricants, so that with great repeated strain it can fulfil its buffer function best.

Defence against pathogens

The connective tissue is even involved in the defence against pathogenic influences such as infections. It goes into action even before the immune system of the body intervenes. The first local defence reaction comes from the tissue hormones. Furthermore the pH value of the damaged body area is moved towards the acid environment. Changes in the injured area ensures that inflammation does not spread any further.

Communication and exchange

The connective tissue is in constant exchange and communication with the cellular elements of the human body. It mediates between the cells and the vascular, lymphatic and nervous system. Nutrients and information are given off to the connective tissue and distributed from there to the cells, so metabolic waste products and information from the cells flow in the opposite direction via the connective tissue.

Biochemical tasks

Mechanical energy – such as pressure, touching – has biochemical effects on the fascia. Hydrogen compounds result from this. The fascia is able to contract and expand again in response to tiny impulses. This mechanism, which is also very important in Bowtech, is the basis of most bio-energetic transformation processes in the body. Methods like the Bowen technique can consequently influence decisively the cell metabolism via the system of the connective tissue.

The connective tissue never forgets

Every trauma, every shock and every situation of stress have their impact on the connective tissue. Scientific studies have shown that the pathogenic process only starts after the receptive and defensive function of the connective tissue has been exceeded. There are many reasons for irritation of the connective tissue. Whether injuries, mechanical strain, physical or chemical processes, traumas or operations – all these are situations of stress for the fascia.

Understanding the muscle structure is an important basis for understanding Bowtech.

If the body receives help in coping with such situations such as with Bowtech treatment, the pathogenic tension in the body can be released

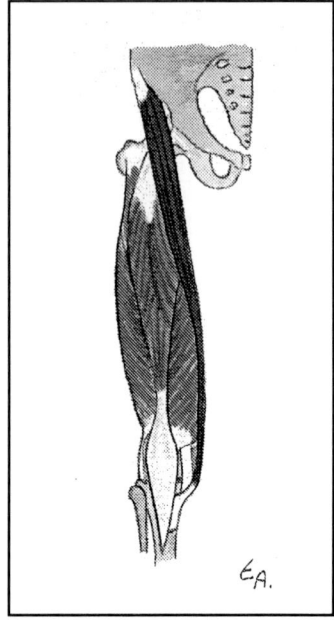

Tension, which remains in the muscles for a longer time, can cause functional disorders or chronic diseases.

again. The lymph flow and the blood circulation as well as the oxygen supply to the tissues are improved, the fascia relaxes increasingly, becomes softer and pain disappears.

If tension remains for a long time and the trauma in the connective tissue is stored on the cellular level, this leads to functional disorders, which can lead to chronic and severe illnesses over the years. The body's system of fascia is also called the body's memory, it does not forget anything. All influences from outside as well as mental traumas are stored therein, as in the file of a computer programme.

Over the years and the accumulation of traumas in the body, the fascia system loses more and more the capability of defence, the possibilities to compensate decrease. In this way the organism is overtaxed more easily and pathogenic influences can spread more quickly. If the energy of the stored traumas is freed and integrated through treatment, it will be at the body's disposal again as defence energy, strengthening the defence system of the organism.

The task of the nervous system

One of the most fascinating and complicated systems of the body is the nervous system. The nerve paths are the transport routes for information in the body. They relay instructions from the brain to the muscles and organs and give feedback to the brain.

A complicated network

The nervous system is built like a tree. The trunk is the spinal cord, which is protected and embedded in the spine and works together with the brain. Starting from the brain and spinal cord, the single nerve bundles extend through the whole body to the ends of the fingertips and tips of the toes, like the branches of a tree. Nerves can be trapped or pressed together due to displaced vertebrae, for example. A crushed nerve can be compared to a river, which is blocked up with stones – information can not flow freely and unimpeded anymore. This causes the body's health to suffer.

Nerve cells are not able to divide or renew themselves as other body cells.

Some of the points found in Acupuncture, Acupressure and Shiatsu are also affected by Bowen technique.

The voluntary nervous system

Human will and con-sciousness control the voluntary nervous system, which reacts to every kind of sensory impression. It is especially controlled via the control centre of our organism, the brain, which secretes hormones via the glands and is involved in the develop-ment of emotions. Some impulses – such as the knee-jerk reflex – come directly from the spinal cord and are not subject to the mind and therefore cannot be controlled voluntarily.

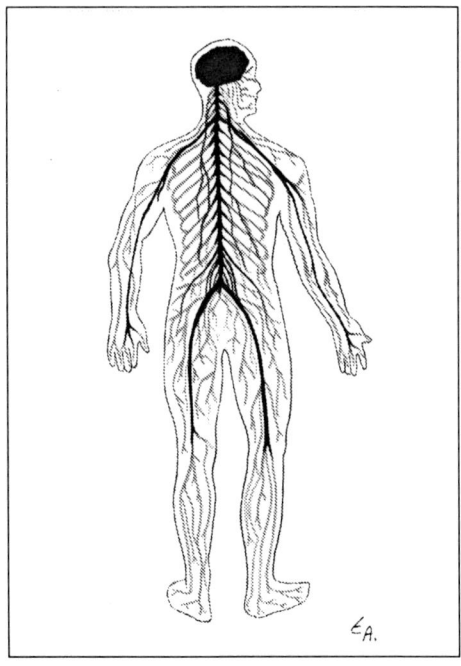

The whole body is connected via nerve pathways to the control centre in the brain.

The involuntary nervous system

The functions of the organs, the heart and blood vessels, the intestines and glands are controlled by the involuntary – autonomic – nervous system. It is independent from will and consciousness and ensures in this way the maintenance of all vital body functions, for instance also during unconsciousness.

Bowtech has an especially balancing effect on the involuntary nervous system.

The self-healing power of the body

The nervous system which works together with the bio-computer brain is considerably involved in the self-healing mechanisms of the body. It transports the healing impulses right into the tiniest cells and "reminds" it of its internal blueprint. Every wound heals itself. The body knows how to form skin cells, how to secrete pain-relieving hormones in case of injuries, fends off bacteria, causes broken bones to grow together again and which matrix of health is carried inside as a model. It is permanently working to counteract destabilizing influences which make it lose its equilibrium. This is also true for illnesses.

"Less is more" is the motto of Bowtech: Even minimal impulses can cause considerable changes in the whole body, if they are set exactly and precisely.

Sometimes the self-healing power can break down due to stress and overtaxing of the body. The flow comes to a halt. Methods like the Bowen technique are able to support the self-regulation of health. They set energy free, make the stream flow again and give impulses to the nervous system to stimulate the self-healing power.

Not only the body's own structure of health supports self-healing, but also the soul and mind. Inner readiness and the will to become healthy, belief – trust in the possibility of healing – and positive thoughts – joyful emotions full of the vision of a healthy body – all this can often work wonders. Energy follows the attention. A principle which can be applied very well to support the body's self-healing power.

Scientific models of explanation

It was never important to Tom Bowen why his technique worked; the main thing was that it did work and had no damaging side effects. He didn't search for explanations, he dedicated himself to its use and to healing. Tom Bowen always knew what was necessary to be done. He had great intuitive understanding of the connections in the body and body functions. His keen powers of observation and sensitive hands enabled him to detect and ease even the tiniest conditions of posture or tension. According to his opinion tension in the tissue always leads to functional disorders in the body.

The obvious success shown by Bowtech has also awakened scientific interest in the method. Numerous medical studies are concerned with researching on this technique. Meanwhile there are different approaches which try to explain the effect of Bowtech conclusively. Probably there is a grain of truth in each of these theories and when viewed together complement each other.

The theory of nerve stimulation

In case of injury the muscles tense up around the area concerned in order to protect it, to immobilize it and support the self-healing power. If the situation continues for a longer time, the fascia sticks together. This limits the mobility of the surrounding tissue and disturbs the blood circulation. Often this defensive position of the body still remains when the injury has long been healed. The fascia still "remembers" the traumatic situation and can not relax.

Tom Bowen's motto was: Everything that helps people is allowed – even if there is no medical basis for it.

The explanation model of nerve stimulation assumes that Bowtech sets a nerve impulse, which activates the communication channels of the body – from the single nerve paths to the brain. The receptors for such impulses are situated in the connective tissue, in the fascia. The nervous reflexes enable the muscles to relax and rebalance again, the stuck fascia loosens up, the work of the organs is stimulated and the blood circulation and the lymph and energy flow are stimulated.

The body receives the "all-clear", the danger is over. It is able to let go and remembers its matrix of health.

The vibration theory

It assumes that the rolling moves – the Bowtech moves – create a vibration pattern and therefore specific frequencies in the body. They communicate with other body parts and tune the organism onto a healthy frequency again. Scientific research has shown that ill cells do not vibrate in harmony.

Healthy vibration is harmonic and balanced as far as the cellular level. The body instrument can be re-tuned and set into healthy harmonic vibration by Bowtech, which largely stimulates and supports the healing process.

80% of all back and neck pain disappears after only a few Bowen treatments. These conditions are often caused by incorrect posture and bad sleeping habits or not enough exercise. For long-lasting, sustained relief these patterns should also be changed.

The stress release theory

Emotional conflicts and traumas create stress in the body, which impair the autonomic nervous system. This leads to stress situations and a reduced capability for the body to regenerate itself and recover. The stress release theory assumes that Bowtech reduces stress in the body by balancing the autonomic nervous system. The hypersensitivity of nerves and related muscle tension decreases, pain disappears and healing begins.

The meridian theory

The knowledge about the meridians comes from the Far-East medicine. They consider meridians as energy conductors, as control systems between the physical, the emotional-mental and the spiritual body. According to this view, illness arises from an imbalance within the fine-material bodies, which drops down to the physical body level and manifests there in the form of symptoms. Acupressure and acupuncture have an effect, among others, by stimulating

Many clients report a sense of wellbeing and relaxation after correction of painful old injuries and restoration of mobility.

the meridians and the energy flow in the coarse material body and in the fine-material areas of the aura, the energy field.

Some series of Bowtech moves are applied along meridians and thereby equalize the body energy balance. This theory also explains why various moves on one point often cause effects on a completely different part of the body.

Body, Mind & Bowen

The effect of Bowen technique via the meridian system is also the basis of a new development within the method, which has been taught under the title "Body, Mind & Bowen" for several years. Anne Schubert and Margaret Spicer, Bowtech instructors from Australia, have worked out specific series of moves for disorders of the respective meridians and the related symptoms and illnesses. "Body, Mind & Bowen" accesses the emotional-psychological realm and consciousness and is especially suited for problems which have their roots there. According to the knowledge of TCM,

Bowen can enhance an individuals feeling of wellbeing. Bowen is an extremely useful therapy in those suffering from addictions.

the traditional Chinese medicine, every meridian is not only connected to an organ or organ system, but also related to one of the five elements, wood, fire, earth, metal and water. Emotions are also classified in these elements. So it is possible to make a connection between the meridians, symptoms and weakened body parts and possibly involved emotions and psychological themes.

The wood element

Liver and gall bladder are related to the wood element. According to the science of the five elements, they may be weakened, among others, by very strict up bringing in the past. Also part of the wood element is the fear of failure and loss of position, the need for

Inner balance and homeostasis are the prerequisites for ideal health. Psychological and physiological stress cause imbalances in the body. This causes the body to become vulnerable and therefore prone to disease.

Spring, morning, east, green and wind are related to the wood element.

respect, freedom and independence as well as emotions like anger, rage and frustration. Expressions from the vernacular like "My blood is boiling" also show the connection between emotions and the body. If problems occur in the relevant body parts, the possibly related themes can be addressed and considered as potential triggers of an illness or a symptom.

The fire element

The heart, small intestine and pericardium (heart sac) as well as the so called "triple heater" of the body belong to the fire element.

Summer, midday, south, red and heat are related to the fire element, among others.

Rejection in infancy, scorn, put downs, suppression and the feeling of being unloved can have a lasting effect from the past and weaken the fire element. Also the fear of disgracing oneself and falling out of favour, the need for love,

> *Positive stress creates a healthy kind of tension and supports activities. Negative stress often expresses itself as tension, pain, high blood pressure, annoyance, anxiety and depression.*

self-esteem and admiration as well as desires belong to the fire element and have an influence on the organs and body parts of this element.

The earth element

Stomach and spleen are related to the earth element. From the past, for example controlling, manipulating parents, who triggered off feelings of guilt, can have a weakening influence on this element and the thus related body parts. Also material insecurity, overthinking and worries impair the earth element. Fear of poverty, extreme changes and upheaval as well as the need for material security also belong here.

Late summer, afternoon, centre, yellow and humidity are related to the earth element, among others.

© alle CreativeCollection

Autumn, evening, west, white and dryness are related to the metal element.

The metal element

Lung and large intestine are related to the metal element. As themes from the past, separation, grief and rejection can play a role with problems in this area. Fear of loneliness can weaken the metal element as well as mourning and fear of the future. The need for communication also belongs to the metal element.

The water element

Bladder and kidneys belong to the water element as well as the sexual organs. In these areas, past influences such as domination or abuse by others, sexual abuse, fear and insecurity can have a

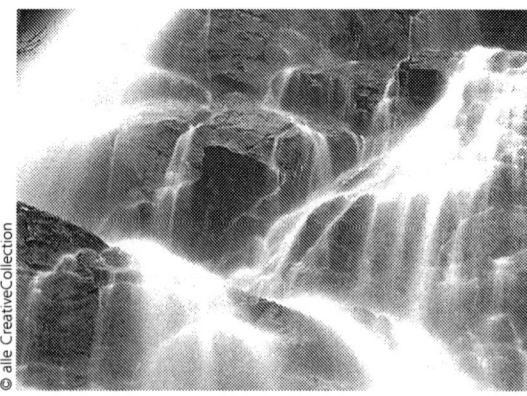

© alle CreativeCollection

Winter, night, north, blue-black and cold are related to the water element.

weakening effect. Also anxiety in general and the fear of not being able to cope with a situation without support,

The five elements are in a continuous change. Each of the five elements represents emotions, tastes and states of heat concurrently.

are subjects of the water element and can have effects on the organs also related to this element. "I go to water", the vernacular says. This element also includes the need for closeness, emotional security and support.

Differences to the original Bowen technique

Less is more, with Bowtech in general, with "Body, Mind & Bowen" especially. The Bowtech practitioners are particularly encouraged with this approach to give the body enough time for self-healing and to allow the clients to feel the body sensations after the individual moves. The basic moves in particular can trigger a strong response. Possible reactions are sensations of cold or heat, tingling or other sensations. Sometimes images of the past arise when old traumas loo-

The body itself gives indications by its reactions, which body parts need to be treated - and when to proceed. This inner intelligence leads the practitioner to the area requiring attention. It determines the pace of self-healing thus avoiding over treatment.

sen; the cause of tension and pain becomes clearer. The next move is not made until the reactions in the body disappear. The break between the moves, which allows the integration of self-healing impulses to the body, can last two minutes with "Body, Mind & Bowen", but also 22 minutes or even longer. This is a clear difference in this approach to the original Bowen technique, where a maximum of ten-minute breaks are made.

The principles of Bowen technique

Bowtech consists of unspectacular small moves and series of moves, which have extremely powerful effects despite their minimal impression. The person's fingers carrying out the treatment surf over the body, ride on small muscle waves and apply gentle healing moves. The organism integrates the self-healing stimuli during the short breaks in the course of treatment and in the consequent days.

©CreativeCollection

How to perform the Bowtech moves

Touch is a language which bodies understand all over the world. It is international and does not need translation. The body is an instrument which translates the touches to impulses for action. With the Bowtech moves, which is what the therapeutic touches are called in Bowen technique, the nervous system receives a gentle but very effective stimulation for a self-optimization of the body.

The matrix of health

Destructive patterns and crystallizations can be loosened, all the stored and often traumatic body memories. Bound energy is set free, the heart and consciousness answer. Everything is connected to everything, the whole system of body-consciousness. Bowtech supports the body to retune itself to its optimal form within the matrix of health.

In contrast to many other methods, Bowtech works with muscle movements, which run transversally to the muscle fibres and in this way trigger off very effective deep relaxation. All moves can be performed on the body as well as through light clothing. The client lies on his/her stomach on a massage table, head to one side and arms alongside the body. The therapist stands on the left. The treatment either starts on the left or the "better" side of the body. It serves

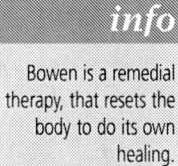

info

Bowen is a remedial therapy, that resets the body to do its own healing.

as a model for the injured or weaker side. During treatment the position is sometimes changed. Various moves are performed lying on the back or even in an upright or sitting position.

The Bowtech move

The gentle gliding and wave-like movement, which is performed over the whole body when using Bowen technique, is called "move" in the original text. It is a matter of a simple movement of the hand, which gives an impulse to the organism and stimulates self-healing. Every move is composed of several sections or sequences, which merge.

Bowtech helps the body to balance itself to its original structure, creating a state of health.

Touch
The stretched fingers or the thumb are placed without pressure on the centre of the muscle prominence, the nerve cord or the tendon, the correct starting point is made by touch.

Slack
The fingers or the thumb produce gentle pressure downwards and forwards, just so much as would be pressed on the skin of closed eyelids.

Challenge
Skin is drawn back gently, like the movement of preparing for the forthcoming movement to the front, and it is held under slight pressure for a moment. This stimulates the fascia and the body receives the signal: "Attention! Something important is going to happen. Please be attentive!" The skin is only drawn back as far as is done easily.

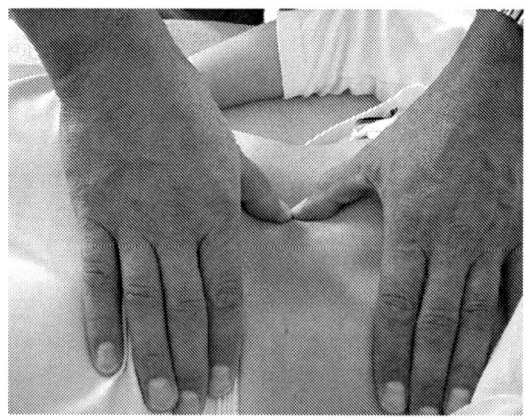

Every move is adjusted to the client's individual tissue tension resulting in a gentle- eyeball pressure move.

Rolling

Under slight pressure downwards a pushing movement to the front is performed over the centre of the muscle, the nerve cord or the tendon. The fingers or the thumb glide as if moving over a bump and thereby feel the tissue clearly under them. The muscle, nerve cord or tendon springs back. This sends a message to the nervous system and the body responds. It starts to react and communicate.

> *Bowtech moves differ from massage moves on the one hand by using hardly any pressure, and on the other that the relevant body part is only touched once.*

The fact that the message has arrived can be proved to the practitioners, among other things, by a kind of electrical impulse in the fascia and be felt by the hands.

Correct pressure is crucial at this movement. Too much can be painful and counter-productive, because the body then closes up and is not receptive anymore. A special, instinctive feeling is required.

Another move follows then or a break after several moves in order to let the body integrate what it has just learnt.

The inner attitude

Careful, attentive, sensitive – that is the way treatment with Bowen technique works. It usually lasts 20 to 40 minutes. Those who come to Bowtech should feel in safe hands, having arrived in a positive healing atmosphere. Silence and peace during treatment, sometimes gentle music for relaxation and hardly any verbal conversation usually characterize a session. The intention and inner attitude, with which treatment is performed, however, is just as crucial as the correct performance of various series of moves and is indicative of a good therapist.

The body reacts to the moves and gives feedback, the practitioners assess the changes in muscle tension or skin quality and from this determine, if the message has been recieved. With a great deal of feeling, inner attentiveness and readiness to pay complete attention to the person on the table, they support the body in its self-healing work. The breaks between the moves have an important role in this as well.

Breaks for integration

Some moves, then a break of two minutes at least – Bowtech seems minimalistic. Anyone experiencing treatment for the first time can hardly believe that so little can be so effective. Between the moves, the practitioners move away from the table, sometimes even leaving the room to let the client's body integrate the set impulses in peace. Every influence on the energy field could have disturbing effects, conversation during breaks could desturb the deeply relaxing atmosphere. The practitioners however usually stay in the room with children and elderly people.

info

The training to become a Bowen practitioner takes about a year. In basic training seminars students gain working knowledge, which they are able to put to immediate use on themselves and others.

Leaving the room could be confusing, children could feel left alone. So before treatment starts, an explanation of what is going to happen with Bowen technique is always given. The duration of breaks can also vary – according to the client's state of health. Up to ten minutes break can be required for integration. Immediately after treatment slight dizziness can occur when sitting up. In this case it is recommended that the patient should remain sitting for some more minutes and then lie down again for another ten minutes if dizziness continues. In this way the effects of the treatment can continue, the body is able to integrate for a longer time until dizziness disappears.

After treatment

The Bowtech effect also continues after treatment. The moves have their effects for as long as one week. The body can be assisted during these days to complete its work. Therefore it is helpful to follow some guidelines:

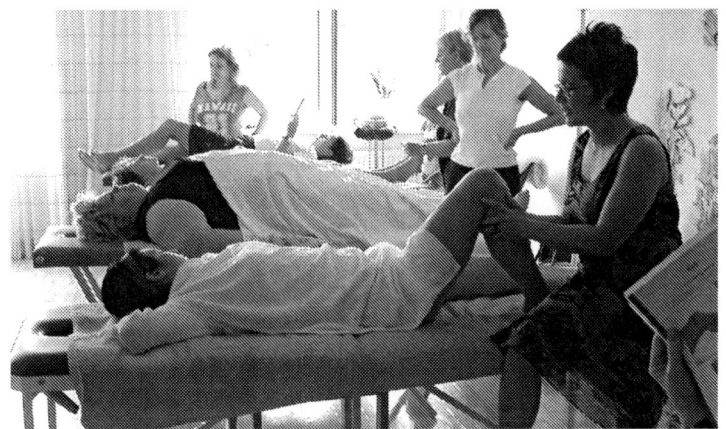

Active application is given priority with Bowtech. The technique can only be experienced in this way.

Stand up on both feet

During and after Bowtech treatment it is possible that even a displaced hip joint and uneven pelvis are realigned. In order to keep this effect and so muscles and ligaments can consolidate in the healthy position, it is recommended to continue to stand up on both feet at the same time e.g. when getting out of bed in the morning or out of a car during the day.

> *The waiting periods between moves give the body time to process the information given.*

Not to sit longer than 30 minutes

Immediately after treatment moderate activity – e.g. a walk – supports the body best while integrating. If sitting can not be avoided for a longer time, for instance while travelling home, the sitting period should be kept as short as possible. Some steps are sufficient to move the body, e.g. a stopover with the car, stretching and walking around the car. A cramped body posture could block it and make treatment ineffective. You should also avoid crossing your legs. This can displace the hip joints, which realigned themselves after treatment by standing up on both feet at the same time.

No exhausting activities

Whereas some activity is good, you should avoid undue strain after treatment. Body building or fitness training can be counter-productive and affect a successful outcome during the first few days. Hard physical work, jerky movements and a lot of pulling on muscles and tendons

Natural activities such as gentle jogging help the body to realign itself.

– such as by a dog on a lead – or a lot of stress and conflicts disturb the body during integration. It should be possible to be calm without lying down or sitting completely immobile.

You should allow yourself breaks and time for relaxation during the daily routine and not hurry back to the office immediately after treatment. Bowtech is highly effective, which is often underestimated. Tiredness and the need for sleep after treatment are completely normal.

Drink a lot of water

Pure water helps the body to remove accumulated waste products better. In some cases distilled water can have a supporting effect. Bowtech stimulates the lymph flow and eventual toxic substances should leave the organism as fast as possible. Drinking large

©CreativeCollection

Still mineral water or distilled water is better than carbonated mineral water.

amounts of water over several days after treatment – at least one and a half litres distributed over the day – helps the body to cope better with pain symptoms and to eliminate waste products and toxins more easily. Concerning nutrition Tom Bowen sometimes recommended taking in 80% of alkaline-forming and only 20% of acid-forming food.

No hot and cold baths

All treated body parts should neither be exposed to great heat or cold. Heat and cold have an effect on muscle tension and can impair the success of Bowtech. For this reason you should avoid very hot baths or showers and also alternating hot and cold applications. Cold or hot packs as well as liniments are not recommended for a few days after treatment.

No other body therapies
Bowtech does not influence other therapies negatively, but supports them, however it is possible that other forms of treatment interrupt the body in its integration work after Bowen technique. Therefore practitioners recommend it is better to avoid other body therapies such as massage, physiotherapy, acupuncture etc. for five days after treatment.

Tom Bowen believed in other forms of therapy, however he recommended limiting oneself to one therapy at a time.

Exercises to do at home
In some cases simple exercises may be necessary to support treatment. It is important that they are actually performed regularly as recommended in order to guarantee the best success of treatment. Such exercises can be, e.g. 20-minute walks combined with special and individual exercises for the back and shoulder area. Some Bowtech practitioners also recommend Yoga, Tai Chi or Pilates. Such exercises stimulate among other things the lymph flow.

Too much of a good thing however can impair the success of treatment as well as not enough exercise. The right quantity is prescribed by the practitioners after treatment and should be observed.

Do the recommended number of exercises and in the sequence given. Do not over exercise. This will enhance the success of Bowen treatment.

Possible healing crises

Bowtech can trigger off a crisis of healing such as other natural therapeutic methods. If some symptoms increase after treatment for a short time, it is a sign that the body is responding to treatment and that healing has begun. Healing crises can occur, but not always.

aboutpixel.de©goenz

The Bowen Technique enhances an individual's feelings of well being by reducing tension, this often occurs within a very short period of time.

Tiredness and sleepiness are also possible as well as vivid dreams during the first 24 hours after treatment.

Due to the increased detoxification of the body it can happen that the nose starts to run or a slight headache or raised tempe-

Healing crises are signs that the body has accepted and acted on the set impulses, even if they sometimes can be a bit uncomfortable.

rature occur. In such cases it usually helps to drink even more, preferably clear water in order to remove roughage, similar as in fasting. After brief discomfort initially, long-lasting pain or old reoccurring disorders often disappear suddenly all at once and forever, usually one or a few days after treatment.

The body regenerates itself after tension and blockages have been loosened up if enough vitality is there. Blood circulation, the lymph and energy flow as well as the flow of the nervous energy improve. The renewal of cells run at full speed, the whole organism restructures and rebalances itself because Bowtech stimulates the body's selfregulation. This process can last from a few minutes up to several weeks.

You should not be worried about healing crises. In the long term lasting well-being prevails after treatment. The foreseeable positive effect of treatment usually makes a temporary crisis more easily tolerable.

The most important basic Bowtech moves

The so-called basic treatment – originally called BRM (Basic Relaxation Moves) – is usually the start of a Bowtech appointment. It is relaxing for the back and the neck. The treatment performed on the spine and the nerves housed within it, has its effects on the whole body and especially stimulates the energy flow and detoxification.

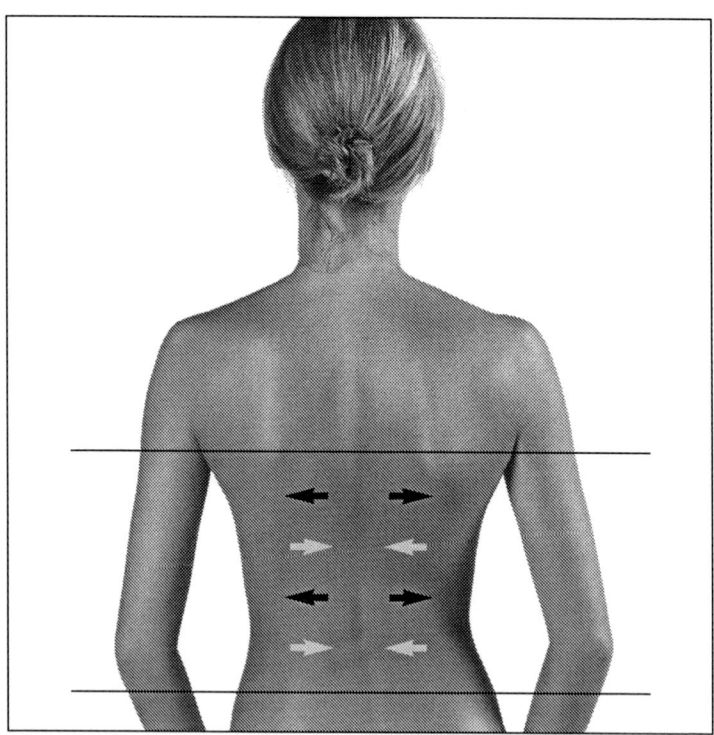

Basic treatment and further steps

The basic treatment on the lower and upper back as well as on the neck helps the body to reduce tension, which is situated especially in these areas, and to assist energy to flow better again. Furthermore it has a positive effect on the equilibrium of the body.

Via the spinal nerves in the vertebrae the whole of the body with all its inner organs can also be reached. 50% to 70% of problems can be solved with the basic Bowtech moves.

Supporting the body

Some of the basic treatment moves on the lower and upper back are also called stoppers or energy blockers. Their function is to isolate the body part which is between them. In this way the body can concentrate completely on the specific area, without wasting any energy in other areas of the body. Vibrations which are produced by each individual move develop their greatest possible effect in the limited area and so loosen the tissue and musculature even more effectively. The healing power can spread completely.

info

A basic treatment begins the process of clearing blocks in the body. As a result every organ and structure in the body can operate more effectively.

The "lower stoppers" act at the lower part of the backbone, where the spine curves outwards. This part works like a shock absorber in our lives and absorbs many vibrations during everyday life, which could otherwise endanger the more delicate vertebrae above. The musculature there is also stronger and more solid. However, due to daily demands the lower back is usually under stress. Tension, energy blockages and pain are often the consequences. That is where Bowtech begins with the basic treatment of the lower back. The sequence of moves is essential for all treatment. In Bowen technique we always work from the lumbar to the shoulder area, never the other way round. Moves performed in a different sequence could trigger off undesired reactions.

The correct Bowtech moves and their effects have to be studied in courses.

The described sequences of treatment are not recommended for imitation, but should only serve for a better understanding of the method. This is not a textbook – experimenting with moves without training and the wrong sequences of moves can, in severe illnesses trigger off undesired symptoms! Bowtech is completely safe – if the method is applied correctly. Learning the Bowen technique – even if it is only for one's own use – requires a sound training.

The basic treatment of the lower back

In the first Bowtech appointment the basic treatment of the back is of primary interest. It relaxes the whole body and prepares it for further special moves. You could say, the field is ploughed before the seeds can be planted. This is the task of the basic Bowtech treatment. It causes a lot of energy to flow, which is blocked in the area of the back, making further work easier for the body. In order to continue the metaphor: Seeds in loose earth can come up a lot more easily

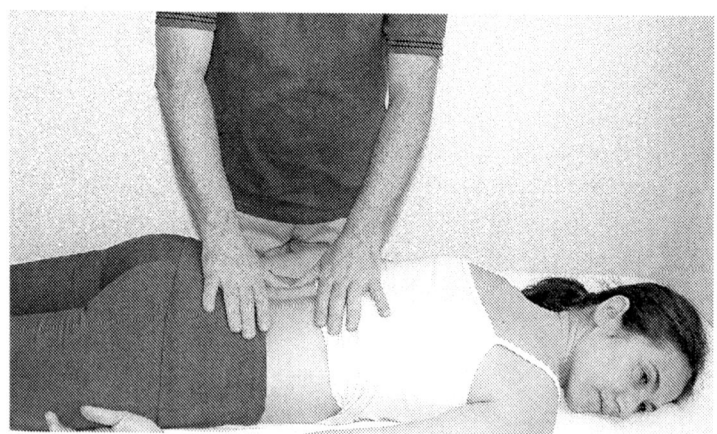

The body reacts instantly to an applied move – unlike massage, where points are massaged longer.

than in hard earth. The back muscles sometimes are stiff from tension, which finally loosen with the Bowtech moves.

The treatment of the lower back starts with the lower stoppers. They are also repeated before performing some other sequences of treatment and moves in the lower area of the body.

The lower stoppers

The therapist stands at the side of the patient to be treated, who lies on their stomach. He or she puts both hands with the thumbs touching each other on the back muscle along the spine above the hip bone. The thumbs pull the skin slightly outwards and then press them gently on the outer edge of the muscle. They remain there before moving with slight and continuous pressure over the muscle to the centre of the body. The first "move" has been performed. Without changing his or her position, the therapist repeats the same move on the other side of the body. Instead of the thumbs this time the tips of both index fingers are used.

In the beginning a lot of concentration is needed to feel the different muscle responses. Gradually the experienced practitioner can easily recognize which muscle groups are not in balance.

Further moves for the lower back

After the lower stoppers the next moves follow on the upper side of both big gluteal muscles. The thumbs pull the skin slightly back and then roll back to the muscle edge with slightly increased pressure back again.

The big gluteal muscle also influences the hip and knee by interacting with the hamstrings.

After this move the therapist changes to the other side of the body and repeats the same move on the second gluteal muscle. This sequence of moves also loosens the muscular layers below. It is followed by the first break in treatment of at least two minutes.

Four moves on the legs

After the integration break further treatment starts to loosen the lower back with the outer hamstrings, which lead down to the knees. The finger tips of one hand are placed in the middle of the gluteal fold below the buttock, the thumb of the other hand rests on the opposite end of the muscle above the back of the knee. The muscle shows

The waiting periods between the sequences of moves are fix elements of the treatment. Clients often become very relaxed and sleepy.

– with successful application of the move – a reaction at its upper end, which can be clearly felt by the holding fingers.

Then the thumbs are placed in the middle of the outer hamstring, another Bowtech move follows on this place. Consequently the therapist changes again to the other side of the body and carries out both moves once again in the opposite direction. This is followed by another break of at least two minutes.

Back to the buttocks
After the moves on the legs and the integration break both moves on the upper side of the big gluteal muscles are repeated. The basic treatment of the lower back is concluded with a move, which is called the "hit the lat" and is part of the treatment of the knee.

"Hit the lat" in conclusion
The patient turns onto their back. A bolster or a pillow can be put under the knees, if lying in this position is uncomfortable. The thumbs start on the outside of the knee and perform a Bowtech move. The same move is repeated on the other leg. The work on the knees has effects up to the lower back.

The Basic treatment of the upper back

This middle part of the basic Bowtech treatment is the bridge between the treatment of the lower back and of the neck. The basic treatment is always performed in exactly this sequence. Whereas the

Bowtech moves should never be painful and should always be gentle.

treatment of the lower back has positive effects on disorders in the lower spinal area, the basic treatment of the upper back helps against pain and tension in the shoulder area and with breathing, chest and diaphragm problems.

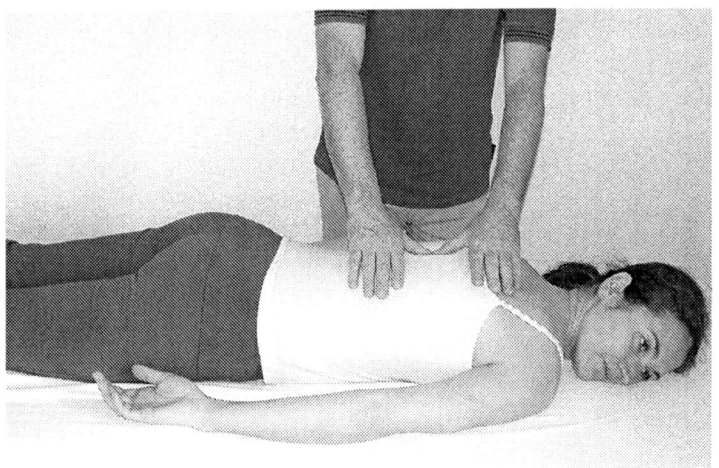

Bowtech treatment can also be performed through clothing.

The upper stoppers

The client lies again on his or her stomach, the therapist stands at his or her side. The first four moves of this basic treatment act as stoppers also. Therefore both hands of the therapists with the thumbs touching each other are situated between the spine and the lower part of one of the shoulder blades. Starting from this position the first move is performed. Then the same move is carried out by the fingers on the other side of the body. The same move follows again on the left and the right some centimetres higher. Then a break of two minutes supports the body in digesting the moves.

During treatment the Bowen Therapist should watch to ensure the patient does not become cold. If necessary, cover with a blanket or towel to keep warm.

Two semi-circles above the shoulder blades

Both moves that follow the break seem like the shape of a boomerang. The fingers of one hand are situated in the middle of the trapezius muscle, the thumb rests on the shoulder blade. The index finger of the other hand is placed below. During the move the thumb draws a semi-circle, which reminds one of a boomerang, diagonally across the muscle.

After having finished this move the fingers stay on the shoulder, continue along the upper edge of the shoulder blade and prolong the drawn boomerang a little further. The same movement is carried out on the other side of the body. Then the body is allowed to rest and respond for another two minutes.

info

The cause of tension is often not situated where you feel it. For example a lopsided pelvis position can be responsible for tension in the shoulder and neck area. Therefore treatment of the whole body is recommended.

If the muscles between the shoulder blades are still tense, the basic treatment moves for the upper back can be repeated. Before doing so it is possible to carry out two additional opposite moves on the lower edge of the shoulder blade.

The middle of the back

Now the area between the lower and the upper stoppers is divided into four segments of the same size. In the lower quarter a Bowtech move is set on the left and on the right side of the spine. In the second segment the same moves are repeated in the opposite direction a bit higher. Then moves of the same kind follow in the third and fourth section.

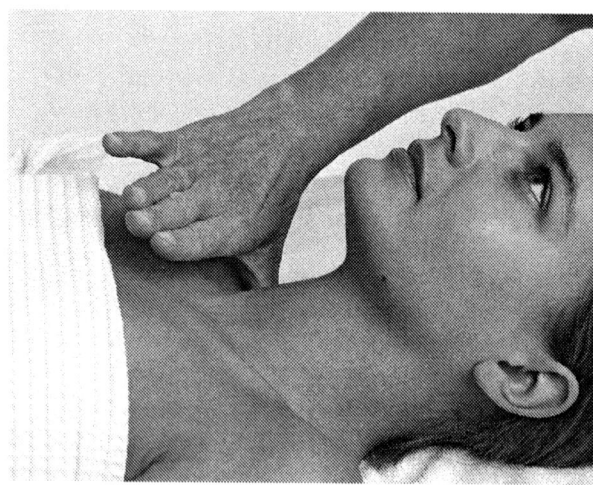

Moves on the neck are part of the basic treatment. They help to loosen neck tension.

The Basic treatment of the neck

This sequence of moves helps with all muscle and skeletal problems in the area of the neck and shoulder girdle. Like the basic treatment of the middle of the back as well, it especially stimulates the energy flow and leads to a detoxification of the body. For the basic treatment of the neck the patient turns onto their back and puts their arms next to the body. The head can rest on a pillow, the therapist stands or sits at the upper end of the treatment table.

Moves on shoulders and head
One of the thumbs is placed on the neck. Starting from there it moves along the neck line across the muscle cords to the front of the body. Then the same move is carried out with the other thumb on the opposite side of the body. Then one hand moves diagonally under the client's head and the middle finger applies a Bowtech move. The same move is repeated with the middle finger of the other hand, before the body is allowed to have another two minute break.

Since treatment of the neck stimulates the elimination, it can also help constipation.

Two moves on the neck
Now one finger feels the upper part of the trapezius muscle on the neck and a Bowtech move is applied. The same move is also performed on the other side of the neck. Then another two minute break follows before these two moves are repeated.

Treatment of the whole body

Bowtech is not a treatment of symptoms and not a treatment for illnesses. It treats the whole person and helps to find the balance of the body and energy system. Therefore further steps after the basic treatment are usually not limited to single body parts.

Most treatment starts with the basic treatment to loosen the body. Then different specific combinations of moves can be used. However,

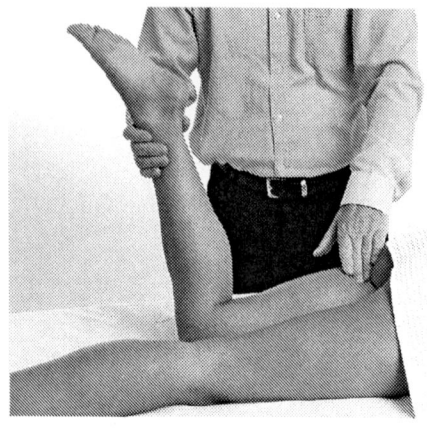

Tension in the femoral musculature is often partly responsible for back pain.

in the work on the knee for instance, the calves, thighs and ankles are included in the work.

Knee and back of the thigh

Treatment on the knee is carried out for all kinds of knee complaints and can also help to loosen muscle spasms in the muscles of the calf. It starts with the knee treatment, which can also contribute to good recuperation after knee operations, among other things around the patella, along the muscles of the calf and on the Achilles tendon. The treatment on the knee is also effective in connection with the shoulder and the ankle.

Treatment on the knee also has effects on other body parts, such as the lower back, the shoulder or the ankle.

Whereas knee treatment is carried out lying on the back, the client lies on the stomach again for treatment on the thigh. The lower legs and the feet are also included in the Bowtech moves on the thighs.

Particular to this treatment is a little punch with the closed fist on the balls of the toes. This gentle "shock treatment" leads to even deeper loosening of the muscles. Of course injuries or osteoporosis (reduced bone density) are taken into consideration. First of all the foot is turned in a circular movement clockwise and anticlockwise at the ankle for about five seconds.

After working on the foot in the course of the thigh moves a five-minute break occurs.

The kidney area

As with all alternative and complementary methods it is recommended that you ask your doctor before starting Bowtech treatment in case of an illness. The Bowtech moves in the kidney area are very helpful and supportive for very different symptoms in this area, however they do not replace traditional medical treatment.

The client is treated lying on the stomach for the kidney moves. The moves are applied on the lower back on the left and right side of the spine. During treatment the leg on the opposite side to the performed move is bent and slightly turned outwards, while it is held by the therapist.

Pelvis and sacrum

Work on the pelvis is performed lying on the back and also includes the knee with the "hit the lat" move. Since this move is performed very close to the pubic region, close to the groin, it is important that everything is explained exactly before treatment.

The more blocked an area of the body has been, the longer it will take for the signals to be interpreted by the body.

Another move on the pelvis is carried out with one leg raised with the hip flexed. The therapist moves the knee to the opposite shoulder, bending is performed only as far as feels comfortable.

Prior the pelvic treatment, tension of the inguinal ligament is tested. If pain or tension occurs in the sacral region during this test, treatment is also recommended. For this the client stands bent forward with the legs as wide as the shoulders, hands resting on the massage table. The legs are straight, the pelvis stretched away so that a hollow back is formed. Treatment is carried out on the lower end of the sacrum. The sacral treatment can also be performed independently from the pelvis treatment. Pregnant women especially feel its beneficial effect with back pain and it can be carried out on them without hesitation.

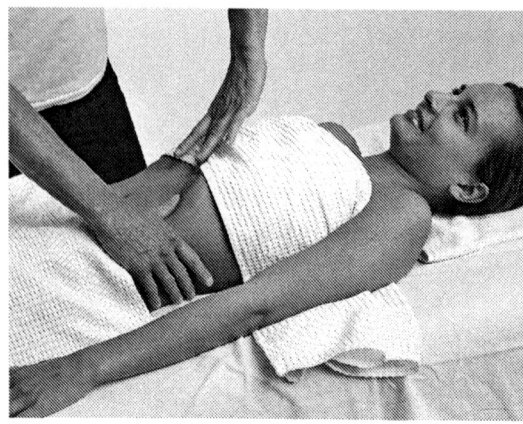

The treatment of the costal arch loosens the diaphragm - and with that a large muscle as well.

The respiratory system

Treatment of the respiratory system is carried out lying on the stomach first, then on the back. This sequence of moves can, among others, have a beneficial effect on asthma, bronchitis or hay fever, however it does not replace medical treatment in such cases.

Bowtech moves can provide help in acute cases of illness and symptoms in the respiratory system.

During the Bowtech respiratory treatment a leg is bent at the knee and turned out. While the client is breathing in and out deeply, a move is applied close to the shoulder blade. On the front of the body – i.e. at the lower edge of the ribs and between the costal arches – a move is applied at the end of the outbreath. This helps the body to relax and let go, using the power of breathing to support the moves.

The treatment of the respiratory system can also be carried out for acute colic and with newborns or infants having stomach cramps or symptoms of asthma. Children are sometimes held by an assistant during treatment.

The gall bladder region

After treatment has been carried out two or three times on the respiratory system, treatment of the gall bladder to support this area is also possible. Furthermore this treatment is considered to be helpful with digestive disorders. Treatment of the abdominal area is performed lying on the back.

Upper respiratory tract and jaw

Treatment of the upper respiratory tract and the jaw is used for jaw misalignment and many other disorders in the teeth and jaw region. Teeth pushed together into an incorrect position can be corrected by this. Therefore caution is needed with inlays or other substantial dental restorations, because dental adaptations may become necessary as a consequence of treatment. The therapist will point this out to you before applying these Bowtech moves and resolve all relevant questions.

For the moves on the upper respiratory tract and the jaw the client lies on the back, the therapist sits at the upper end of the massage table. The first two moves are perfor-

Symptoms of a misaligned jaw often respond quickly to Bowen.

med on the lower side of the jaw, the next two in the area of the thyroid cartilage at the neck. Then treatment is continued on the top of the breastbone.

Specific to the treatment of the upper respiratory tract is "rocking the windpipe". This means that the windpipe is gently touched on the side of the neck and slightly moved to and fro. Then a series

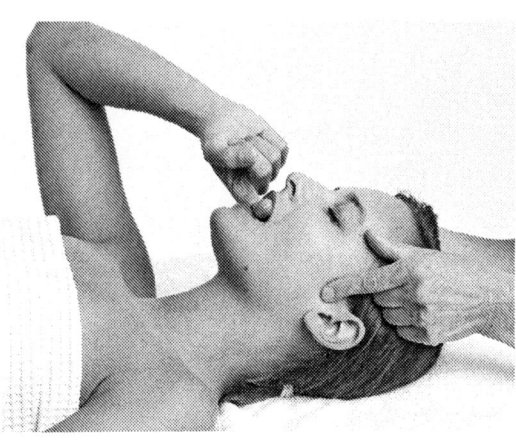

A soft bite on the finger joint stabilises the jaw.

61

Some nerves which affect the lower body region are also stimulated by treating the jaw.

of moves are performed starting from the sternum to the outside of the neck. These moves are also referred to as "milking", because the thumb and index finger move up and down as in a milking movement. These milking moves are repeated up to three times. After every sequence of moves a five to ten-minute break is made.

When treating the jaw, the therapist touches the dimples in front of the cartilage of the jaw joint. The client is asked to put his or her own index finger between the teeth to stabilise the jaw. This is followed by a series of moves along the jaw joint to both ears.

Headaches can have many causes: muscular tension, displacement of vertebrae, digestive disorders amongst others.

Treatment for headache

With this sequence of moves it is not possible to remove the cause of a headache, but pain can be relieved to a large degree, because they contribute to relaxation in the head area. The client lies on the back, the therapist is at the upper end of the treatment table.

During this treatment four points are held with single fingers on each side of the upper region of the head – at the root of the nose, the insertion of the eyebrows, above the forehead and at the temples.

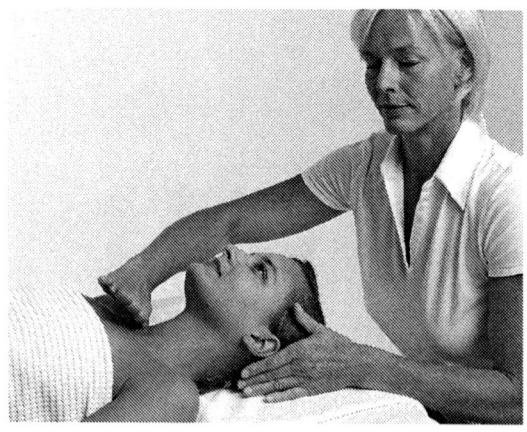

A headache often has its cause in the area of the neck.

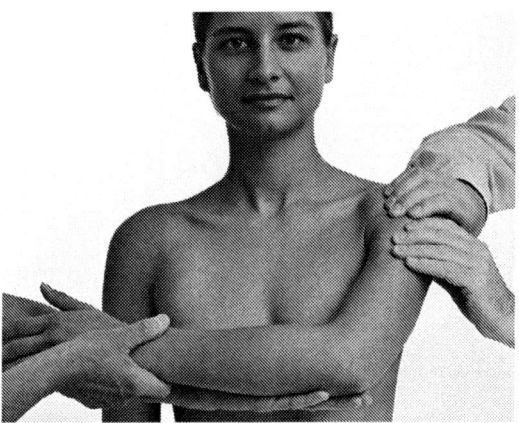

With the help of assistants the therapist is able to perform the move more effectively.

The series of moves is repeated four times. Finally the balls of the thumbs are placed on both final points at the temples, where they maintain constant pressure for some seconds. This is followed by a 10 to 15 minute break. The treatment for headache is only treatment to relieve pain. Consequently the causes such as tension in the neck or digestive disorders need to be treated.

Shoulder, elbow and wrist

The moves for shoulder treatment are performed while the client is standing. In most cases an assistant helps during treatment to support the arm and bring it into different positions.

Bowtech also supports rehabilitation after operations.

Furthermore the assisting person also feels the reactions of successful moves in the form of vibrations and informs the therapist. He or she stands behind the patient and applies the moves, while the assistant stands in front of the person. In the sequence of moves on the shoulder there is a small slap as a specific requirement as well, which is carried out with the ball of the thumb on the outer side of the upper arm below the shoulder joint. This consolidates the moves on the shoulder. If no assistant is available, treatment on the shoulder can also be carried out alone. In this case the client sits on a chair with a back rest, the therapist stands in front of him or her.

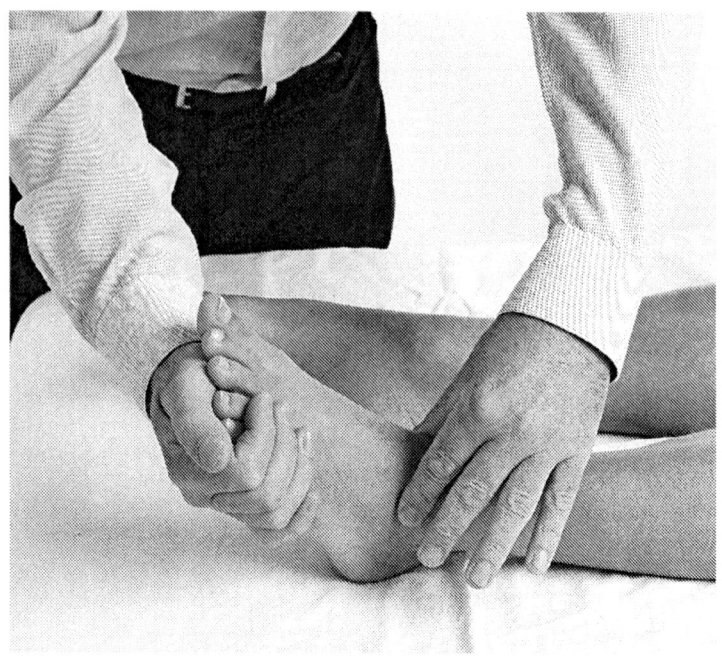

Blockages in the ankle often inhibit energy flow along the relevant meridian.

The elbow and wrist are also treated in a sitting position, while the hands lie loosely in the lap. The Bowtech moves for these areas are also possible lying on the back with arms relaxed. During treatment on the elbow the arm is bent and supported by the therapist. After the first move on the forearm the middle finger shows a slight reaction due to the interplay of the muscles and proves that the move has been performed correctly and effectively. When treating the wrist it is also bent with the help of the therapist. A loose "shaking out" follows at the end of the treatment on the hand. The elbow is thereby carefully moved in circles first, and then the relaxed arm is slightly stretched, which aligns the wrist.

A great deal of sensitivity is needed, particularly for deformed body parts such as the hallux valgus. As soon as the patient feels the touch as unpleasant, pressure should be reduced.

Ankle, hallux valgus (bunion), hammer toe

The client lies on their back during treatment. The therapist holds the foot which is to be treated bent upwards, while he or she performs the moves on the ankle and the forefoot. At the end of the foot treatment, the foot is rotated at the ankle for some seconds. Finally the therapist gives a short abrupt punch on the ball of the foot.

By the treatment of the hallux valgus several Bowtech moves are performed around the metatarsophalangeal joint. The therapist stretches the big toe as long as tension feels comfortable.

A frequent cause for infertility is poor circulation in the abdominal region.

For the treatment of hammer toe he or she carries out a series of moves repeatedly on the sole of the forefoot. The pressure of the fingers is gradually increased, however only as long as is comfortable for the patient.

Infertility

Tom Bowen developed a special programme for couples who are unable to conceive. First of all both are balanced with basic treatment. In cases of irregular menstruation treatment of the coccyx is carried out until the woman's menstruation has become regular. Then the couple are treated with the coccyx move again one day before menstruation. Then two weeks of sexual abstinence is necessary before sexual intercourse can be enjoyed again around ovulation.

Often only a few treatment sessions prove successful. If not, the programme is repeated before the next menstruation.

Possibilities for self-treatment

Bowtech is not really a method for self-help. In an acute situation some moves can be applied easily to oneself. Even if these moves are not performed correctly one hundred percent, they cannot cause harm but, in the worst case simply do not help. However we strongly advise against experimenting with Bowtech moves.

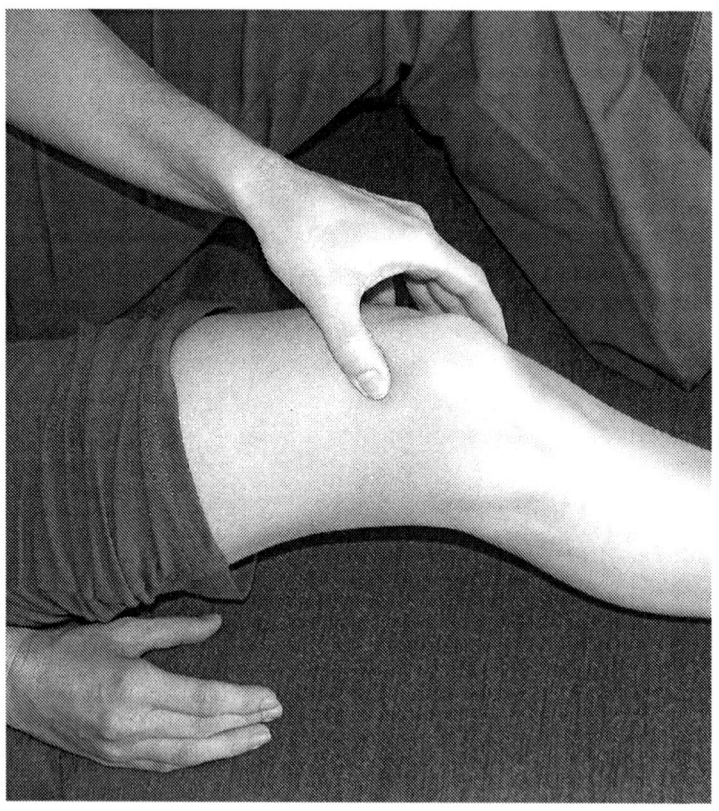

Self-help at home

Whether moves on one's own body, exercises to support treatment or recipes from Tom Bowen's medicine cabinet - the Bowen technique also offers a lot for use at home. However, you should not experiment with other moves as described in this book, because improper use can have undesired adverse effects. The sequence and direction of the moves is also always crucial.

Helpful moves for the acute case

This book does not replace a Bowtech course and is not suitable for self-study. It should only convey a greater understanding for the basics of the technique and the way it works. Nevertheless some moves can be used safely at home and in an emergency. They should be used immediately, so they have very quick and effective results. With more serious injuries and severe symptoms you can at least relieve pain until medical treatment.

info

If you want to use Bowtech for self-treatment, you should attend a course in order to become more experienced. Even if you cannot harm the body in the long run, the efficiency of moves requires a lot on practise.

Loosening of the neck

With tension, muscular and skeletal problems in the area of the neck it can be helpful to carry out a move from the basic treatment of the neck. These moves loosen and stimulate the energy flow of the body. You start on the neck at the upper part of the trapezius muscle on the area between the earlobe and the shoulder – on the left side with tension on the left side of the neck, on the right with tension on the right side.

The finger tip of the left middle finger is situated in the middle of the band of muscles on the left side of the neck. First pull the slack skin outwards a little, then using gentle pressure with the finger on the outer edge of the muscle, move the skin slowly and under constant pressure towards the spine.

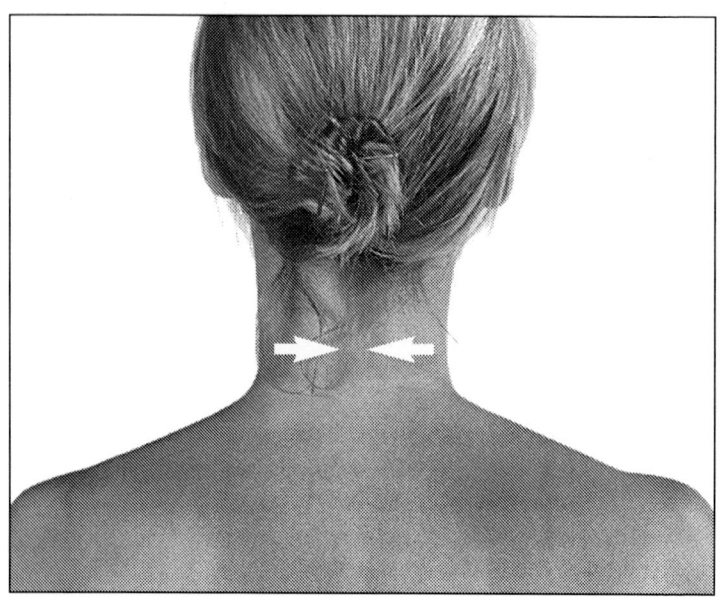

Neck tension is very effectively treated by the simple neck moves.

The same move is carried out on the right side of the head with the right middle finger. If necessary, the move can be used on both sides of the neck also. It can be very effective with early morning neck tension, but can also help with headache, restricted movement in the neck and dizziness.

"Hit the lat" for the knee and back

The "hit the lat" move on the knee, which also finishes the basic treatment of the lower back, does not only loosen a painful knee, but also the whole area of the lower back. It can be carried out in a standing or sitting position with elevated legs.

Self-treatment of the neck also helps with dizziness, headache and restricted movement in this area.

The knee is slightly bent and relaxed for this move. Usually this is easier in a standing position. If the muscle is under too much tension when sitting, the move can not have an optimum effect.

Place the thumb on the side of the knee above the tendon, approximately one to two centimetres away from the patella, first pull the skin gently back and finally move very slowly with a

The knee is connected to the whole body via the fascia.

sure move over the muscle as far as the patella. The treatment on the knee stimulates the energy flow and is very good for complaints during or after playing golf, hiking or other sports, if the knee is overstrained.

Lower stoppers with back complaints

Even only one or two moves often lead to significant relief of symptoms.

The stoppers on the lower back can be used in self-treatment in a lying or standing position. They help with complaints in the back and small of the back and serve to loosen and stimulate the energy flow. To do so put both hands above the hip bone on the body with the palms on the body. The fingers are stretched out and pointing towards each other,

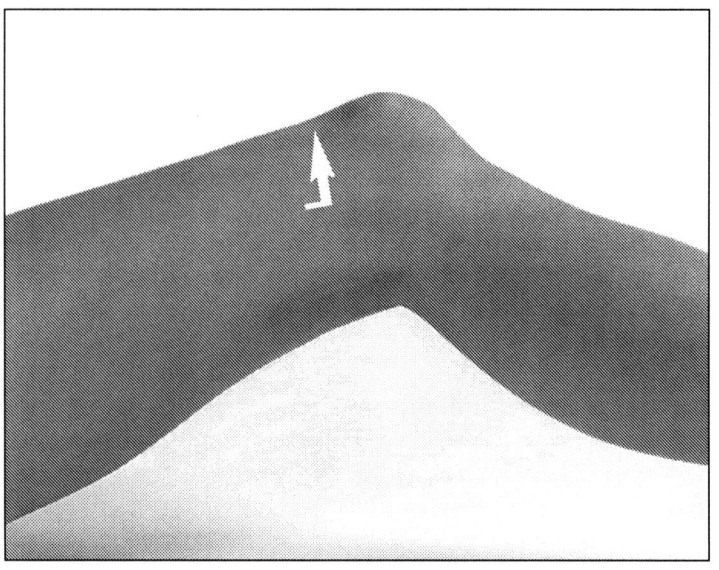

The self-therapy moves on the knees provide relief for painful knees after hiking, skiing or golf.

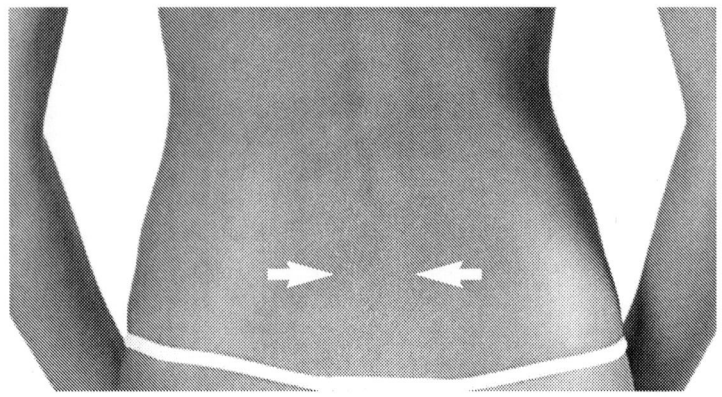

Of all the moves, moves on the lower back quickly bring about deep relaxation.

the finger tips are placed on the longissimus muscle on the left and right of the spine.

For the move on the left side of the body the fingers pull the skin slightly outwards, press on the outer edge of the muscle and stay there for three seconds before moving to the centre of the body under continuous pressure across the muscle. The same move is performed with the right hand on the right side of the body. This self-treatment is very effective in bed before going to sleep in the evening.

Liver, gall bladder, spleen and stomach also benefit from this treatment.

These moves have a calming effect on the whole body. Before going to sleep they relax the body and can lead to a better night's rest. In this way tension or pain in the whole back can often dissolve over night.

Move for problems with the respiratory system

The following move can lead to relief in the respiratory system in case of allergies, hay fever, asthma but also with seasickness, hiccups, nausea, feeling of fullness after meals, heartburn, upset stomach and flatulence. It may also be used for colic in children and newborns with digestive disorders.

The move is best carried out in a relaxed position lying on the back.

The thumb is placed between the costal arches, the fingers on the lower costal arch. While breathing out the skin is pulled upwards with the thumb and after this movement of drawing back it is pushed downwards. This move is also called the emergency move, because it loosens the diaphragm in case of acute breathing difficulties and as a result facilitates breathing.

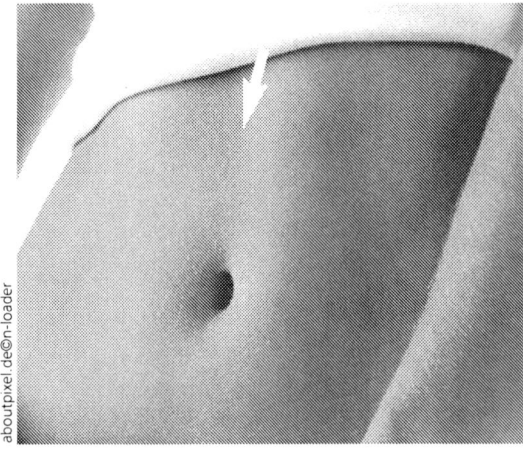

This move leads to a loosening of the diaphragm and improves the blood circulation in this area.

aboutpixel.de©n-loader

Problems which can be helped by Bowen technique

Back pain, sprained ankles, knee problems, migraine, stress or anxiety, are just a few of the problems that Bowen technique can address. People of all ages from infants to the frail and elderly can be treated, as well as animals. Healing often takes place with astonishing results.

aboutpixel.de©broller

When Bowtech – when not?

The Bowen technique has many uses and there are hardly any reasons for exclusion. This is probably one reason why the technique has spread so quickly. There is hardly any illness, hardly any symptom, hardly any person or animal that cannot be treated successfully.

Who is Bowtech suitable for?

The list of those who Bowtech is not suitable for is far shorter than the list of those who can experience healing and relief. At the very least an improved sense of well-being can be achieved. In some cases of severe illness this means already quite a lot. Bowtech is also used in patients with Parkinson's disease or multiple sclerosis, for example, or after a stroke, with muscle atrophy or facial paralysis.

Chronically ill people and handicapped people often experience a significantly better quality of life and relief of pain by

> **info**
>
> Generally Bowtech is suitable for almost everybody – from the infant to seniors, from the healthy to the ill person. Astonishingly good success has been achieved with sport injuries or after operations – here the healing process has been improved significantly.

Bowtech. The method is also well suited to support medical treatment. The recuperation time after operations can also be reduced. In this chapter you will find some examples of people and animals that could benefit from Bowtech.

Healthy people

Prevention is one of the slogans of our time. Health care should prevent illness more and more instead of treating complaints in case of an illness. Those who are balanced, become ill less frequently. Bowtech rebalances the body, strengthens the immune system, increases well-being and the energy balance, so it is perfectly suited for harmonization, relaxation and prevention of illness.

Tom Bowen, a keen basketball and football follower, successfully treated many injured players on the sidelines. For this he earned instant praise and his reputation as a healer was well known.

Pregnant women

Pregnancy often leads to unpleasant accompanying symptoms such as back pain. Here Bowtech provides relief by sacral treatment. Only the coccyx must not be treated with pregnant women, otherwise all moves are allowed and beneficial.

The most frequent conditions treated with Bowtech

- Sciatica and back pain
- Sprained ankles
- Knee problems
- Tenosynovitis
- Frozen shoulder
- Stiff neck and whiplash injury
- Jaw problems and grinding of teeth
- Stress and hypertension
- Irregular menstruation and PMS
- Pregnancy complaints
- Migraine
- Menopausal complaints
- Organ problems
- Bronchitis and asthma
- Allergies and hay fever
- States of exhaustion
- Dizziness
- Bed-wetting and many more

The gentle, non-manipulative Bowen moves, can be used on neonates. Parents and therapists are often surprised at the infant's quick response to the treatment.

Newborns, children and elderly people

Age is no reason to exclude Bowtech treatment, neither too few nor too many years. Since the Bowen technique is very gentle and applies only small but very effective body moves, it can be used in newborns and infants as well as in elderly people without hesitation.

Newborns, children and also animals usually respond immediately to treatment and often do not need any breaks between the moves to integrate. They react without expectation or refusal, and often only require a few shorter or lighter moves to rebalance them. Midwives who are experienced in Bowtech can carry out the necessary moves on newborns with birth traumas even in the delivery room and so make it easier for the little body to release the trauma. The treatment is also helpful for colic or restlessness. Infants are often treated on the floor instead of on massage tables and beds, sometimes even while they are playing and in the presence of their parents.

Babies with teething or colic problems respond well to Bowen treatment.

With elderly people with osteoporosis, for example, the moves can be carried out even more carefully and gently in the region of very delicate or fragile bones. There are no reasons to exclude treatment.

Amateur and professional sportsmen

Even the sports fan Tom Bowen knew about the fast and de-trau-matising effect of his moves on sportsmen and -women. Football players in the team Tom Bowen cared for, who were injured during the game, were very often fit enough to carry on playing after only a few Bowen moves.

If Bowtech treatment is carried out imme-diately after an acci-dent, the body recu-perates in an astoni-shingly short time.

Bowtech moves which are carried out immediate-ly after an accident often prevent a manifestation of the consequent trauma to the body. Swelling and other consequences of an injury can often be stopped or considerably reduced by a few moves if carried out straight away. Thanks to Bowtech treatment the recu-peration period after accidents is furthermore considerably reduced.

With Bowtech to the world champion's title

Mario P. reports:

Peter Knoll (note: The under-mentioned Bowtech practitioner is neither related to the author nor related by marriage) convinced me in November 2003 by his competence, humour and gentle hands – this was when I became Powerlifting World Champion in England. The Powerlifting World Championship in Mexico (26th to 28th Nov. 2004) was a particular challenge for us not only due to the distance and the time difference of eight hours. Twelve days after treatment had started I fell badly ill with the flu, so that I even had to go to hospi-tal with suspected meningitis. The Bowtech therapy plan was changed only once: "Concentration on the upper part", Peter said, and this short intervention did not only have an effect on the upper region – that is to say the whole system was cleaned thoroughly within 24 hours. Our eyes started to shine clearly again and we continued working together. Thousands of kilos per training session, correction of the movements, absolute discipline even in nutrition and Bowtech. An ideal programme for a huge success was realized step by step. This led to a dramatic increase of performance, high elasticity, much reduced recovery periods, no injuries and no illnesses.

With hints, confidence and the words: "We have tried our best, listen to your feelings and trust in yourself", Peter said goodbye. The flight via Paris to Mexico City-Chihuahua lasted 16 hours (the total journey took more than 23 hours!).

On the day of the competition my reliable travel alarm clock woke me up at 5 o'clock in the morning, after a 4-hour sleep – the world champion was reminded of his warm-up sessions; superlative performance was expected!

Due to preparation work in the competition hall and the large number of participants, I

Tom Bowen was above all known for his effective treatment of sport injuries.

had to wait 14 hours until my first attempt. Tiredness, the difficulty of determining the right moment for the intake of food in this phase and, related to this, the danger of a huge loss of power let first doubts about success arise. The tense atmosphere was furthermore penetrated by announcements, groans of competitors and the hectic cheering of the coaches.

During these hours, in which we were condemned to wait, I remembered Peter's farewell words. The hardest weeks of my life were behind me: innumerable sacrifices, strain that even a sportsman in peak condition cannot imagine. However I also enjoyed champion like Bowtech moves, performed by an ever present friend. And this treatment also let my impressions grow again. Joy spread through me and

The world champion's title 2004 – despite of severe flu! For Mario P. definitively the result of hard training – and Bowtech.

info

Especially in competitive sport the danger of injuries is high and personal form on the day decisive in a competition. Therefore it is not surprising that many sportsmen all over the world like to entrust themselves to the hands of experienced Bowtech therapists in order to increase their fitness.

eliminated every negative thought. I was sitting there beaming like Siddhartha by the river: relaxed, concentrated, perceiving everything but leaving me untouched. At this moment my body remembered its real state - information and energy pulsed through me.

With a never before experienced confidence I succeeded in my tries: bench pressing: 120 kilograms, back lifting 190 kilograms, knee bend 200 kilograms. 3 disciplines, 3 world records and the title of World-Champion 2004.

At the airport, even David Carter, the first world champion in powerlifting history, praised my perfect flow of movement. What more is possible?

The World Championship 2005 in Germany is waiting and we will make up the best team in the world once again! Muchas gracias!

Mario P.

Further reports of success

Bowtech is versatile and has an effect on many varying complaints. There are a large number of case histories and enthusiastic reactions.

Several patients, suffering from migraine or trigeminal neuralgia, have reported astonishing success thanks to the Bowen technique.

A small extract from the innumerable reports of success follows.

Sciatica and headache

For about 35 years I have, at times, suffered from agonizing sciatica, which has been made bearable with ointments and medication. After years of sedentary work on the computer I also had severe neck tension, which could neither be relieved by massages nor by specific gymnastics. Consequently: migraine and a headache almost daily. As if that wasn't enough; I then slipped a disk, which increased the continuous pain; this was treated by injections and electric therapy,

Constant daily pain can make life miserable. Bowen offers a way out of this situation.

pixelio.de©karin schmidt

short relief and then the pain returned. I was tired of treatment with tablets and appointments with doctors, when I heard of Bowtech. After the second treatment my continuous pain was considerably reduced. After five treatments I have now been free of pain for over four months! Thanks to this method my life has become worth living again.

Gerda A.

Painful menstruation and back pain

I repeatedly suffered from unbearably painful menstruation and had to take two or three tablets nearly every month in order to be able to stand the pain. After about four treatment sessions I am now almost symptom-free. I find the Bowen treatment very relaxing and pleasant. My back pain, which I used to have due to my job, has disappeared for some time after the Bowen treatment. I am surprised again and again how fast and efficiently this therapy works.

Andrea Sch.

"Mouse finger"

As a student at a computer-orientated college I often have to write on the keyboard and use the mouse for many hours. For this reason I was not surprised to get the so-called mouse finger. I had enormous pain and could hardly use my right hand anymore. I tried protective

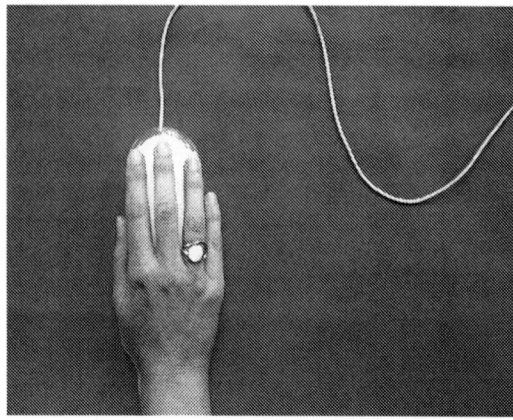

Using the computer for long periods of time or performing repetitive tasks – leads to tension and pain on one side of the body.

therapy and sports liniments, however nothing helped. Then I heard of Bowtech and underwent treatment. The same day after the first therapy I already noticed astonishing relief and the next morning all complaints had disappeared as if by magic.

Doris B.

Pain in the jaw joint

At the end of my studies I was suffering from pain in the right jaw joint for months. The symptoms started slowly with occasional difficulties, e.g. biting off a piece of bread or apple. I felt as if I wasn't able to open my mouth enough and had furthermore the impression that my chewing muscles were continuously losing their power. Consequently I was only able to partly open my mouth or I could only open it asymmetrically. I often woke up in the morning not only in constant pain, but also with tension in the area of the muscles of the floor of the mouth and the neck muscles.

Time to do something about it! Besides orthodontic treatment in form of splints, pain therapy, physiotherapy, I had the opportunity of enjoying a Bowen technique session thanks to friends. Generally open to alternative methods of treatment, I was able to gain a symptom-free state to a great extent just after a few treatment sessions.

Sabine G.

Histamine and dust allergy

I suffered from a severe histamine and dust allergy. After wrong food and wrong drinks my mucous membranes became badly swollen and my nose started running heavily within five minutes. During the night I could not breathe through my nose and on getting up in the morning I had very severe sneezing attacks (20 to 30 times). In winter I caught one influenza infection after another due to these problems.

Success rates with allergies means a healthier constitution and a stronger immune system.

I started treatment. After the third Bowen session I got an itchy rash all over the body, which healed after about a week. From one treatment to the next my symptoms improved. When we finished the Bowen treatment, I could eat everything, drink nearly everything (apart from Prosecco), breathe through my nose during the night and the sneezing attacks in the morning only occurred rarely. I am very glad to have come upon this technique. The quality of my life has largely improved thanks to Bowen.

Petra W.

Depression

My mother, 56 years old, has suffered from depression for about 20 years. The attacks reappear every two or three years. In the past medicine helped; this has not been the case as she has become older. A

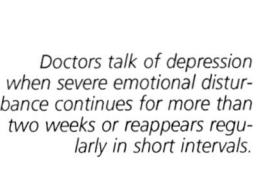

Main causes of depression are, eg. hereditary factors, stress in everyday life and work, continuous failure, lack of relationships and tension in the body.

www.pixelio.de

Doctors talk of depression when severe emotional disturbance continues for more than two weeks or reappears regularly in short intervals.

short time ago I started to use the Bowen technique on my mother, which I had learnt in a basic course. After the second Bowen session, she already felt better. After the third treatment her depression had nearly disappeared and now, after another three weeks, it has completely gone. Of course my mother is overjoyed that the Bowen technique has helped so quickly. Now she is full of life and active again.

Birgit P.

ADS (Attention deficit syndrome)

Our son was extremely restless and had severe concentration problems, which naturally had an affect on his performance at school. The teacher referred us to a school psychologist, who performed some tests: we were then told that our son had strong indications of ADS.

We carried out an appropriate concentration therapy with the child, which did not help at all. Our son did not make any progress, neither at home nor at school. I was also given the advice to give him therapy with Ritalin.

Other methods of treatment have also shown that tension which leads to bad blood circulation, increases or triggers AD-syndrome.

Then I heard about Bowtech through my husband. After the first therapy a kind of counter-effect started: the boy became hyperactive, I could hardly stop him. However during the following days we could notice a significant improvement: He did not forget his homework anymore, he became much calmer, his fits of rage reduced considerably and he listened much more attentively, i.e. now he is also able to carry out several tasks. His concentration has also improved a lot. We are glad to have found such a good solution for our son.

Brigitte B.

Practitioners report

In the network of Bowtech practitioners there is a constant exchange of treatment outcomes from practising the method daily. In this way the possibilities of Bowen technique applications are being continually refined.

Diabetes mellitus

My husband Herbert (54) has been diabetic for 33 years. He tried to regulate his sugar level with tablets, nutrition and sport. It differed a lot depending on physical and mental strain. Despite some low points (long-time level 12) he refused immediate admission to hospital as well as insulin injections.

Since then he has always paid a lot of attention to nutrition (whole food, a great deal of vegetables and salad) and regular exercise, so he has reached a long-time level of 8. I have been treating him nearly every week for seven months. Since he had cold feet as well as problems with his hips, knees and neck, I carried out all possible kinds of treatment during this time, focusing mainly on the respiratory area.

Herbert felt better from week to week, he became more balanced and able to do more. Although he sometimes over indulged during this time, even with sweets, his daily profile became consistently more balanced. He was not troubled

For practitioners the variety of results from Bowen treatments is amazing.

by the six monthly check-up. He did not have any disorders anymore, and even had warm feet. Happily for him, at this check-up the long-term level had been reduced to 6.

Erna Schickelgruber

Jaw regulation

I used Bowen to support the tooth and jaw alignment for my daughter Lisa (11). The upper jaw was too narrow and the upper teeth protruded due to the posterior occlusion in the lower jaw. Lisa got her first dental brace at the beginning of June for the upper jaw which was too narrow, and I started with Bowen technique at that time: basic treatment, upper back, neck, upper respiratory tract and jaw, pelvis and knee.

Under the umbrella of the Bowen Academy, practitioners are able to discuss and exchange ideas relating to new aspects of healing.

We had a break during the holidays and restarted regular treatment at the beginning of the school year. The control of the dental brace in October showed a considerable extension of the upper jaw. So Tina got her second dental brace for the lower jaw five months before the planned exchange (originally the treatment plan was laid out over three years).

Encouraged by this success, Lisa was ready for the next Bowen sessions. I continued changing between jaw, pelvis and knee treatment. We also allowed ourselves a break during the Christmas holidays. At the next check-up of the dental brace in January they also measured the difference between upper and lower jaw. The result was obviously surprising for the dentist, too: the gap had reduced from eight to three millimetres within this short period.

At the moment we are allowing ourselves a short break, as there is the half term vacation. We are already looking forward to the next appointment with the dentist in four weeks. Who knows, maybe Lisa will get her third dental brace.   *Helene Obereder*

Insect stings

Even when she was a little girl, my daughter (9) reacted to insect stings (wasps, bees) with high fever, headache and swelling which spread over whole joints and extremities. The painful swelling often disappeared only after two weeks.

Some weeks ago she was viciously attacked by a swarm of wasps during an excursion. My first thoughts were "helicopter, emergency doctor" - however, we did not have a mobile phone with us and were in the depths of a forest. So I undressed her quickly (there were still some wasps on her clothes) and started to carry out a move below

The toxic poison of bees and wasps can cause allergic reactions, which can be life-threatening, for many people. Bowen offers help in these acute situations.

and above each sting. The stings had already become giant weals. My husband talked calmly to our daughter and started treatment of the stings himself. When we finished with the last sting, the others could hardly be seen anymore. My daughter neither got swollen or feverish. Furthermore she did not have any pain. Without Bowtech our excursion would surely have ended in hospital. In the evening I carried out basic treatment and the kidney moves and I gave her a lot of water to drink. Although she had about 20 wasp

Bowen moves perfor-med immediately after insect stings, allow swelling and inflam-mation to disappear very quickly.

stings, she did not show any reaction. Furthermore she has lost her panic-stricken fear of bees and wasps. A few days ago she showed me two stings on her middle finger, which she had treated herself.

Monika Rei

Tenosynovitis of the forearm

A colleague (32) was suffering from tendovaginitis on the right fore-arm for two weeks. He was under medical care, in great pain and could not hold anything in that hand. The forearm was visibly swol-len. His doctor prescribed tablets and a liniment, which obviously did not have the desired effect. An appointment had already been made in order to fit a Moltopren bandage with a splint to increase the tem-perature in the arm from 5° C to 6° C.

I offered Bowen treatment to my colleague. I carried out the stop-pers for the lower back, then for the upper back, the neck, treat-ment of elbow and wrist and consequently treatment for the car-pal-tunnel syndrome. Furthermore I told him to apply a washing soda pack on his forearm over night. The next day he came to work very impressed and told me that the pain had almost gone. Even the swelling was not visible anymore. The washing soda pack had hardened and could be taken off like a cast. I proposed to apply one or two more packs, but he considered them unnecessary. The only disadvantage, according to him, was that he had not slept very well. After seven days I carried out the same treatment on him; however he was already completely symptom-free.

Rudolf Puchinger

Scoliosis

Mrs S., a student (23) had suffered from scoliosis for several years, however it was never treated. She suffered from increasing pain in the upper back and, when sitting for a long time, she had a great deal of pain at the coccyx, which turned out to be a big problem for her as a student.

Scoliosis, curvature of the spine, often leads to reduced movement and severe pain.

First she received all types of basic treatment and further scoliosis treatment in the following weeks: basic treatment, kidneys, then basic treatment, kidneys and coccyx changing with basic treatment and thoracic procedure etc. Finally she received coccyx alternating twice. After eight weeks the scoliosis had reduced significantly (it had almost disappeared), especially however pain in the area of the thoracic spine and also pain in the coccyx had completely disappeared. This improvement has now continued for a year.

Martina Barelmann

Fulfilled wish for a child

Maria (31) had no greater wish than to have a child for many years. Her partner was of the same view, however unfortunately it remained unfulfilled. Consequently an odyssey from one doctor to another began but

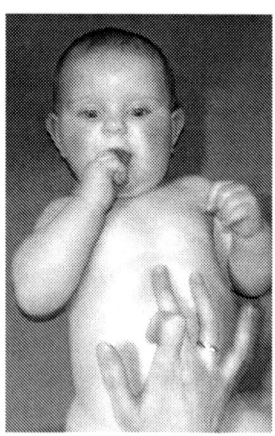

Bowen often helps to solve the problem of infertility.

without success. On the recommendation of a gynaecologist who, after several medical attempts, had experienced a very positive change in his own state of health thanks to Bowen, Maria came to me.

Tom Bowen also had positive results in treating problems relating to infertility.

At intervals of seven days I carried out Bowen treatment on her. The menstruation became regular and one day before the period I performed the basic and coccyx treatment. As already discussed no sexual intercourse occurred until two weeks later. I didn't hear from her for some weeks. One morning there was the surprising phone call: "Inge, I am pregnant!"

Inge Floimayr

A lump in the breast
On 15th January my aunt called me (after we had been working very successfully on a stomach-intestine problem from the beginning of the year onwards), because she had felt a lump the size of half an index finger in her breast and her doctor had sent her to hospital for examination as soon as possible.

I explained the chest moves to her on the phone, which she carried out on the following days. When she told her homeopath on 18th January that she believed that the lump had become smaller, he just advised her to be careful with such statements – often it was just wishful thinking. On 22nd January we carried out treatment: upper back, chest – and the recommendation: to allow oneself to take more time. Finally, on 24th January there was the examination in hospital with the doctor's question: "Why are you actually here? All the results are okay." I have been especially happy about this story.

> The USA has shown great interest in the scientific research being done on the Bowen Technique.

Maria Mierl

Latest results of research

Since the network of the Bowtech practitioners has spread widely in the meantime, the network of Bowtech researchers has spread as widely too. One of the most untiring among those who try to explain the technique scientifically as well is the American doctor and Bowtech practitioner Jo Ann Whitaker from Florida.

She is head of the "Bowen Research & Training Institute" – in Palm Harbor. In her studies as well as from others she shows with the help of several test subjects which symptoms and illnesses Bowtech has been proven to help. A short excerpt is shown as follows.

Fibromyalgia

Fibromyalgia is an illness of the support structures and the locomotor system, which is accompanied by pain and fatigue symptoms in muscles, ligaments and tendons. This is supposed to be caused by reduced energy circulation, which leads to an energy deficit in the muscles. The persons affected have been shown to change myosin into glucose to an abnormally high extent, which is considered the cause of occurring pain and fatigue symptoms. A conventional method of treatment for fibromyalgia has not yet been discovered. The Bowen technique could be a possibility for these patients, which was the starting point of research.

The first studies on the proven effect of Bowen are already in progress – however it will still take several years before all the scientific proof has been collated. Untill then the clients' well-being should be the primary concern.

Joe Ann Whitaker and the rheumatologist Sally Marlowe included the HRV measurement (heart rate variability) into their study with eleven patients suffering from fibromyalgia and a control group of eleven healthy people. With this method it is possible to measure the function of the heart and of the autonomic nervous system as well as changes in these areas. The autonomic nervous system regulates the body's heart function, breathing, hormone system, digestive system and the system of peripheral vessels. In the study it was observed that all functions and body systems, which are influenced by the autonomic nervous system, responded to Bowen technique and were balanced by it.

All persons affected had been suffering from pain for at least three months and received the Bowtech basic treatment. The results of the treatment showed that all those with fibromyalgia observed an improvement of their symptoms. Many even felt great relief which lasted for days or weeks. Further research should help to find out the number and frequency of Bowtech sessions which lead to the best results for fibromyalgia.

Frozen shoulder

A frozen shoulder means any trouble related to painful and severly restricted movement in the area of the shoulder. The loss of mobility for the persons affected lasts at least a month, the pain spreads from

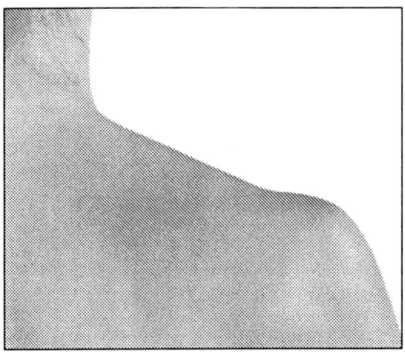

Pain and stiffness in the shoulder can be treated quickly and effectively by Bowtech.

the shoulder to the area of the forearm. For the sufferers the loss of mobility means that they can often only live their lives under limited conditions, with severe pain that frequently leads to sleep disturbance and considerable mental strain.

A study in Great Britain confirms the effectiveness of the gentle Bowen moves to help shoulder restrictions.

The methods of treatment offered are physical therapy and exercise, injection cures, medicine, manipulation of the affected body area under local anaesthetic, electro-acupuncture and so on. Usually healing lasts for a period of one or two years.

The British study by Bernie Carter, which observed the influence of Bowen technique on the symptoms of a frozen shoulder, included 20 test subjects. Six of them each received five sessions of Bowtech treatment, another six received four sessions and the remaining eight came to three sessions of treatment. The majority of them – 13 people – had suffered from pain and restricted movement in the affected shoulder for three months.

Complications such as stiffness in the joints of the knee, elbow or shoulder, usually a result of fractures or surgery in these joints, requires long term therapy to treat the stiffness. The Bowen Technique offers an often quick alternative to these long term therapies.

By the use of Bowen technique 70% of the test subjects reached such a significant improvement after the end of the treatment series that their mobility showed no difference between the affected and the completely healthy shoulder!

The degree of pain was also reduced from very intense pain to just slight pain or completely pain free. The persons affected could follow their daily activities in an almost unimpaired way again and were very satisfied with this gentle form of therapy. Based on this study Bowtech can be considered as a positive possibility of intervention for the above problems.

Carpal-tunnel syndrome (CTS)

In the carpal(= hand)-tunnel syndrome a sensation of numbness, symptoms of paralysis and pain arise usually from the area of the thumb, the index and middle finger eventually spreading as far as the arm. This is caused by lesions of the nerves which provide sensation and mobility to the hand. The concerned nerves are situated under the connective tissue of the wrist surrounded by tendons which form a kind of tunnel – the carpal-tunnel. If this tunnel is too narrow, the nerves can suffer.

Carpal-tunnel syndrome is usually very painful and often leads to a sensation of numbness in the fingers and the arm.

In the course of the illness the muscles, which the damaged nerves supply, can also become weak. Then it becomes no longer possible for example to splay out the thumb or bend the fingers. Consequently the affected muscles become atrophied more and more. The recommended therapy is the positioning of the fingers on splints especially during the night and operations to enlarge the narrowed connective tissue.

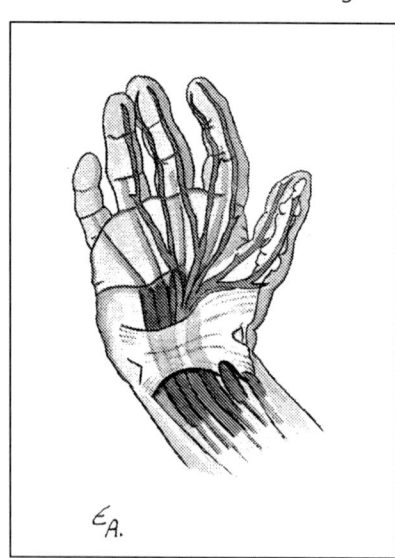

The carpal tunnel denotes the tunnel-like area in the connective tissue of the wrist, which encase the nerves of the hand.

The six persons affected, who took part in the Bowtech study carried out by Glenys Sheedy on the treatment of the carpal-tunnel syndrome, had been suffering from pain and the sensation of numbness in the wrist and the fingers for as long as three years as well as shoulder and neck pains due to hard physical work. One of the participants had restricted movement of the hand and forearm. The test subjects each received four sessions of Bowen technique treatment, one every seven days.

In the course of the study it became evident that the degree of pain and tingling sensation decreased significantly in two patients after only the first treatment. One person could move his fingers the morning after the first treatment and did not feel any pain after three sessions of treatment. In one person numbness and pain disappeared completely after three sessions of treatment for a period of two weeks. In the course of the treatment the shoulder and neck pains disappeared too, as well as emotional problems of the persons affected.

Bowen technique turned out to be a successful alternative method of treatment for three of the six participants and the other three could follow their daily duties, although one of them left the study after the first treatment. One of the successfully treated persons, encouraged by the therapy, overstrained herself with gardening and window cleaning, which led to pain again. She came for another session of treatment.

Restless Leg Syndrome (RLS)

Symptoms of Restless Leg Syndrome are unpleasant sensations, even if they are usually not painful, such as tingling, burning, dragging and itching in the legs, creating a strong urge to move. That is why the syndrome is called "restless legs". Sometimes these sensations can also occur in the arms.

The strong uncontrolled movement of the legs leads to a continuous strain, and increased exhaustion in the persons affected.

Movement relieves the symptoms. With immobility – such as sitting for a long time or during the night – the symptoms increase, so that the persons affected sometimes suffer from sleep disturbance. This consequently leads to tiredness during the day and impairs daily life and personal relationships.

The tingling and itching sensation result in a strong urge to move the legs. It can be triggered, by iron deficiency or poor blood circulation.

About 5% of the population are affected; however the syndrome is not usually diagnosed before middle age or in elderly people. Currently the exact causes are unknown as well as successful methods of treatment. RLS can appear as an independent illness or as a consequence of other illnesses and problems such as iron deficiency, uraemia due to insufficient functioning of the kidneys, polyneuropathy (a disease of the nervous system) and damage to the spinal cord. Usually treatment consists of medication and anaesthetics, which should relieve the symptoms.

The Bowtech study by Marg Biorac from Australia included six people suffering from the Restless Leg Syndrome. One of the persons did not get any treatment and was the control; the other five were treated with Bowtech over a period of four weeks.

All five persons noticed reduction of all symptoms even after the second treatment, regarding the frequency, intensity and duration of the presenting symptoms. One person did not have any symptoms at all after the eleventh day, another after the 16th day and another person was completely symptom-free after the 21st day of the treatment series.

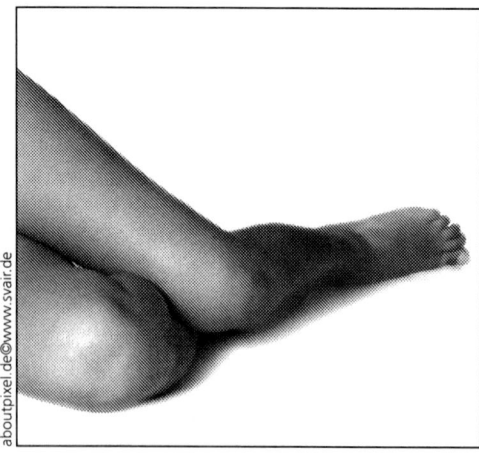

aboutpixel.de©www.svair.de

A study shows that Bowen influences the symptoms of the Restless Leg Syndrome by reducing the frequency, intensity and duration of this disorder.

The remaining two test subjects stated a reduction of frequency, intensity and duration of the symptoms, in one person the symptoms were limited to one leg only.

According to the results of the study the Bowen technique seems an effective method for treating Restless Leg Syndrome. In order to determine more details, longer studies with more test subjects will be required. In any case Bowtech is very suitable as a painless and gentle method to reduce RLS symptoms.

Lymphatic oedema

Eilish Lund examined the effect of Bowtech on lymphatic oedema, e.g. after vein operations, thrombosis or pregnancy. With lymphatic oedema, swellings in the limbs occur due to the reduced lymph flow. Eilish Lund reported about eleven people in her study and stated that most patients' well-being improved significantly with Bowtech, that they moved more freely and –after fatigue at the beginning – began to feel better and better in general.

> *Oedemas are excessive accumulations of fluid in the tissue, which impair its function.*

Over the course of the months she assessed stronger and continuous reduction of the volume of the swollen limbs, e.g. the legs with all patients.

The treatment also had positive effects on the patients' level of pain. In one person pain was reduced after two days; after three sessions of treatment she was completely free of pain. A woman who suffered from severe swelling after an insect sting the year before and from repeated migraine attacks as well, received three sessions of Bowtech treatment over six weeks, after which she was completely free from headache for nine months. To give more detailed assessments on the effect of Bowen technique on lymphatic oedema, however, another study with more test subjects for a longer period will be necessary.

Migraine

About 10% of the British population suffer from migraine. For this reason Nikke Ariff and Janie Godfrey researched the effect of Bowen technique on migraine. The causes for migraine can be hormone variations, food incompatibility, allergies and so on. 39 test subjects participated in the six-week study, 13 of them had been suffering from migraine for one to 15 years, 17 people for 16 to 30 years and the other nine for more than 30 years.

Bowtech can reduce the intensity and frequency of migraine attacks.

During the first two weeks all of them received three sessions of Bowtech treatment, followed by a four-week period to observe the effects. The participants recorded all changes concerning the frequency and intensity of migraine attacks in a diary.

Eleven people noted a reduction in frequency, another eleven a reduction in intensity only, and frequency of the attacks, nine a reduction in intensity, whereas seven people did not notice any change and the frequency increased in one person.

The study has shown that Bowtech can reduce the intensity and frequency of migraine attacks significantly. In total 31 participants stated positive changes with the treatment, which is 79.5% and 36 from 39 test subjects reported that they wanted to recommend the method to others. It becomes evident again and again that the Bowen technique has great success in conditions of pain.

Mental problems and tension

A study by Ashley G. Pritchard from Melbourne, Australia centred on the effects of Bowen technique on mood, heart rate and muscular tension. Ten healthy people – five men and five women – between the ages of 18 to 55 participated in the study.

The following criteria were included to assess the conditions of mood: depression (feeling of personal insufficiency), anger (intense, obvious anger), vitality (feeling of high energy), tiredness (feeling of weakness and low energy), confusion (lack of memory) and body tension. A barometer of anxiety was also made on the basis of 20 questions. Assessment was made immediately before and after treatment and additionally a week later. Measurements of the heart rate (ECG) and of muscular tension were carried out as control measurements before, during and after treatment. Former studies had shown that the fore-

Using Bowen in clients with mood swings must be carried out by an experienced practitioner.

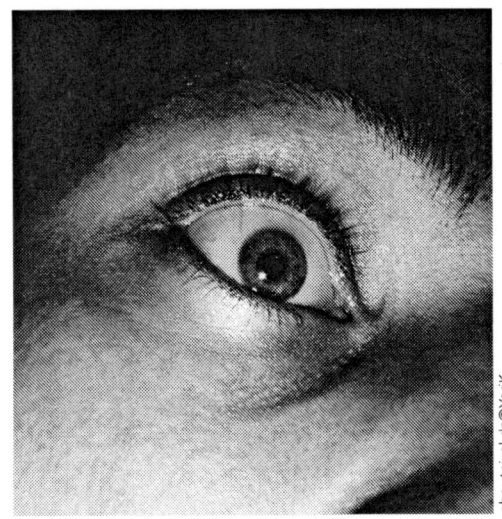

Feelings of anxiety can cause muscular tension. Bowen relaxes the muscles and also effects the emotions.

aboutpixel.de©YariK

head muscle was a reliable parameter to measure general muscular tension and that the relaxed muscle in this area was also accompanied by a reduction of the heart rate.

The study did not show significant differences between male and female test subjects. The test subjects reported for instance a sensation of warmth in various areas of the body during treatment. The data evaluation showed that all increased mood conditions reduced – except vitality, which remained the same or increased slightly. General mental well-being increased continuously after treatment, which was attributed to a reduction of tension, depression, anger, tiredness, confusion and anxiety. For this reason it was concluded that Bowtech is well suited as a method for people who suffer from anxiety, increased tension and other stress related disorders.

This possibility of reducing anxiety and tension could also be used to assist sportsmen and –women before, during and after competitions. As the study proved Bowtech has a reducing influence on the heart rate, blood pressure, body temperature and respiratory rate. Consequently the method helps to achieve mental as well as physical relaxation.

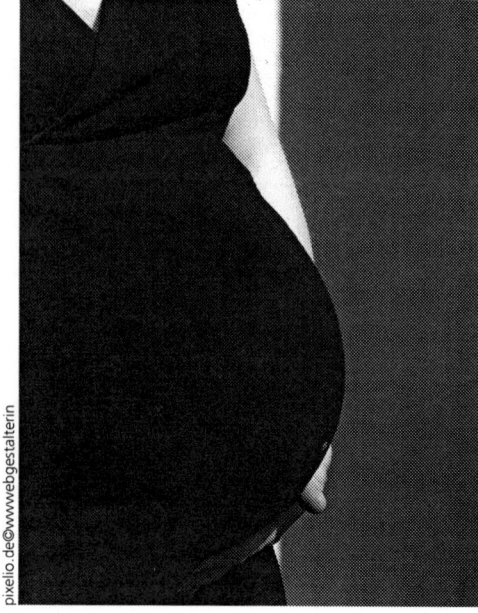

pixelio.de©wwwebgestalterin

During pregnancy a few moves are contra indicated and should be avoided – apart from these, Bowen can be used for general relaxation and well being.

In which cases is caution advisable?

Bowtech can have healing effects for nearly all complaints and be applied on people of all ages.
Only in the following two cases could complications occur. That is why such treatment is avoided.

No coccyx treatment on pregnant women
Coccyx treatment is often performed in the treatment of diarrhoea or constipation and with numerous gynaecological disorders. These moves however must not be carried out on pregnant women.

No chest treatment on silicone implants
Some moves can be applied in the chest area in the case of sensitive breasts. Chest treatment is not performed on clients with enlarged breasts made of silicone.

Bowtech for animals

Although Tom Bowen also treated animals successfully, no instructive records exist about it. This gap was filled by the Australian Alison Goward in 1990, when she developed the E.M.R.T. (Equine Muscle Release Therapy), a therapy to loosen tension of muscles in horses, in short "Bowen for horses". Alison Goward owns horses herself and she is a Bowtech instructor and practitioner.

She applied moves, similar to those used on humans, to the anatomy of the horse and developed sequences of moves, which are now taught in courses to horse owners. The use of E.M.R.T. is intended for the treatment of your own horse and does not replace veterinary treatment, however it can support all other therapies. Training as a practitioner for horses is now possible.

Good success has been achieved with lame horses as well as with injured race horses, show horses or very timid animals. Chills, rashes and infections, hip problems and wounds that are difficult to heal can also be treated. Furthermore the technique is suitable to prevent and stimulate the energy flow in order to keep the animal fit.

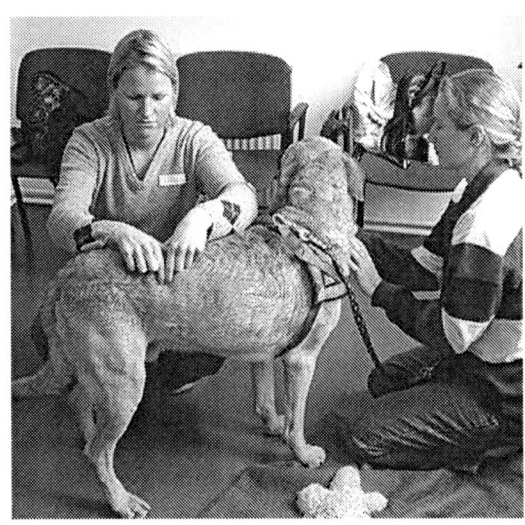

Of course dogs and other pets can also be treated with Bowen. Only a few very gentle moves are usually all that is required.

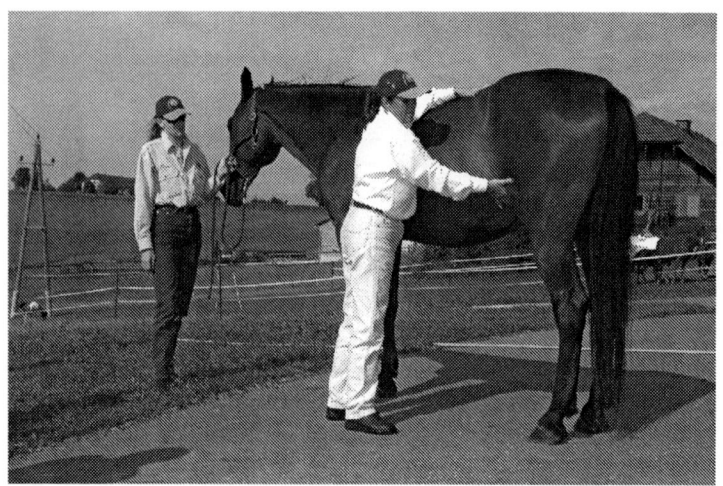

The effects of Bowen on animals, such as racehorses, are astonishing. The method has become quite popular with the racing industry, producing quick results and no need for veterinary medicines.

Apart from horses also dogs, cats and other pets can be treated with Bowtech moves, which have been developed especially for them. This method – Bowtech for pets – is also called CCmrt – Cat and Canine muscle release therapy – and was developed by Alison Goward and Tina Spurling. Some illnesses and symptoms which have been treated very successfully are for instance, arthritis and nervousness. Animals usually respond very quickly and well to the therapy and show a change of behaviour within a very short time. They are often described as especially calm and peaceful after treatment, injured or apathetic animals however can become much livelier than they have been for a long time after "Bowtech for animals", as if new life is put into them again. They usually realize exactly what helps them and keep patiently still during treatment.

Tom Bowen's medicine cabinet

Some home recipes from our grandmothers' times are still very helpful for our health and merit consideration. The same is true for Tom Bowen's hints, which he gave his clients to relieve various discomforts.

Washing soda pack for swelling
In former times the strongly alkaline washing soda was mainly used for washing and cleaning. Today it is still available on the market and can be used for non-inflamed swelling or bruises. Prepare the pack by distributing a layer of about one centimetre thickness in the middle of a handkerchief or a gauze bandage and fold the cloth. Take care that only one layer of cloth is between the skin and the washing soda. In case of swollen knees, the pack is placed directly below the kneecap.

The compress can be fixed with a stocking, bandage or towel, for instance and should be left on the swollen area for at least three to four hours, or better over night. The washing soda can drain off up to one and a half cups of liquid from the body. Small wounds as well as delicate skin areas should be covered with Vaseline, so that the soda does not burn the skin or produce blisters. It is best to apply the pack one day before the Bowtech treatment, in any case not more than twice a week.

Apple cider vinegar compress for inflammation
Cider vinegar has an anti-inflammatory, tissue regenerating and painkilling effect for minor muscle injuries such as sports injuries. The apple cider vinegar compress is prepared by applying vinegar diluted with water on a cloth. Fix a plastic film around the compress.

This compress again should remain on the injured area for at least three to four hours or over night. Use apple vinegar only on areas without skin wounds! A compress will also help with arthritis, burns and colds.

Epsom salts bath for detoxification
For a bath with Epsom salts to detoxify your body, add half a cup Epson salt to the bathing water. The bath should last at least 20 minutes.

Epsom salt is also relieving in case of a hallux valgus (bunion) or calcified joints. One or two dessert spoons for a foot or partial bath are sufficient; the bathing period is 20 minutes.

Bowtech training

The "Bowen Therapy Academy" offers training courses lasting one year, which are composed of several modules. They are attended by people from different care and health professions as well as by non medical people.

Bowtech courses are suitable for non medical people as well as for health professionals.

Different courses offer the possibility to cover any special interest areas.

Further training for practitioners

Those who have finished training at the Bowen therapy academy can also attend several courses for further training. The courses available are:

Bowen for advanced practitioners 1	2 days
Bowen for advanced practitioners 2	2 days
Bowen for mothers and babies	1 day
Body, Mind and Bowen	2 days
Seminar on back pain	2 days
Bowen after strokes and for people with special needs	2 days
EMRT Bowen for horses, level 1	3 days
EMRT Bowen for horses, level 2	3 days
EMRT Bowen for horses, level 2	3 days
CCmrt Bowen for pets, level 1	3 days
CCmrt Bowen for pets, level 2	3 days

Code of Ethics for Bowtech practitioners

All Bowtech practitioners oblige themselves to keep to the following code of honour and to protect the method in this way.

- I will acquaint myself with, and endeavour to adhere to, the code of conduct, guidelines and rules of the association to the best of my ability.
- I will administer Bowtech the Bowen Technique accurately, gently, compassionately and with integrity.
- I will honour and respect the body, mind and spirit of my clients.
- I will use my knowledge and skills to support my clients.
- I will administer the Bowen Technique with the teachings and philosophy of Tom Bowen.
- I will respect the simplicity and power of the Bowen Technique.
- I will respect and honour the confidentiality of my clients.
- I will give hope and assurance to all clients but, will represent the Bowen Technique as a guaranteed cure for any disease, ailment or condition.
- I recognize the power of the Bowen Technique to affect emotional releases and I will be prepared to support those who experience such releases.
- I will make referrals when appropriate and will not misrepresent myself or the Bowen Technique in any way.
- I will respect the wisdom and uniqueness of the Bowen Technique and will not provide, on the same day, any other (hands on) modality.
- I will commit to furthering my skills and understanding in reference to the Bowen Technique by following the continuing education guidelines of the Bowen Association of Australia Inc.
- I will respect and co-operate with any other qualified health practitioner with whom my clients chooses to be involved to the extent that this does not compromise the integrity of the Bowen Technique and/or myself.
- I will co-operate with any ethical investigations instigated by the Bowen Association of Australia Inc. and will report to the association any actions or practices that clearly violate this code.

Appendix

Information & Practitioners

Qualified users of the original Bowen technique can be found and contacted via the Bowtech associations in the respective countries. The original headquarters of the Bowen technique are still in Australia, the management of training within the Australian Bowen Therapy Academy is in the hands of Oswald and Elaine Rentsch.

The Central European training centre, managed by Manfred Zainzinger, has its headquarters in Upper Austria.

The Internet offers easy access to therapists in your area.

Australia
Bowen Therapy Academy of Australia
www.bowtech.com

Central Europe
Bowen Therapie Akademie
www.bowen-academy.com

Manfred Zainzinger

Associations in Austria, Germany and Switzerland offer mutual networks.

Bowen Therapy Academy of Australia
PO Box 733
Hamilton, Vic. 3300
Phone: 0061/(0)/355 72 30 00
Fax: 0061/(0)/355 72 31 44
bowtech@hl140.aone.net.au
www.bowtech.com

United States Bowen Registry (USBR)
337 North Rush Street
Prescott, Arizona 86301
Phone: 866 862 6936
usbr@bowtech.com
www.bowenwork.com

Bowen Association of the UK
PO Box 4358, Dorchester
Dorset, DTI 3FD
Phone: 0700 269 8324
office@bowen-technique.co.uk
www.bowen-technique.co.uk

Bowen Therapie Akademie
(for Central Europe, German speaking countries)
Baumannweg 3
4203 Altenberg
Phone: 0043/(0)/72 30-2 06 78
Fax: 0043/(0)/72 30-7 09 37
bowenakademie@bowtech.at
www.bowen-akademie.com

About this book

About the authors

Manfred Zainzinger was originally a restaurant owner, heard of the Bowen Technique whilst training in remedial massage in Australia. He then met and trained with Oswald and Elaine Rentsch, the directors of the Bowen Therapy Academy of Australia which has become a world-wide organisation.

He then ran a busy Bowen practice in Cairns Australia, became a Instructor with the Academy in 1995 continuing on to become a senior instructor and examiner. He taught the Technique throughout Australia and New Zealand before returning to his homeland, Austria.

Since 1998 has dedicated himself to bringing Bowtech to all the German speaking countries in Europe. He has single handedly been responsible for the success of Bowtech in Austria, he established an Austrian office, edited and produced a German edition of Bowen Hands, then quarterly journal of the Bowen Academy. He was instrumental in establishing an Austrian practitioner association and initiated the formation of the German and Swiss Bowtech associations.

Sabine Knoll is a freelance journalist, author, seminar leader and Reiki master. She lives in Austria and is specialized in the field of "holistic health" which is the balance between body, soul and mind. In the field of informative books her book "Die Dorn-Methode. Verblüffend einfache Selbsthilfe gegen Rückenprobleme" (Mosaik bei Goldmann) has been published.

Note

The advice given in this book has been carefully considered and selected by the authors and the publisher; nevertheless no guarantee can be given. Any liability of the authors or the publisher and its representatives for personal injury, damage to property and financial damage is excluded.

Index

IMPRESSUM

Production and Publishing: Books on Demand GmbH, Norderstedt
Medical specialist advice (eastern and western medicine): Dr. Sathya Bernhard bin Saîf;
Photos: Horst Stasny, Günther Wohlschlager;
Illustrations: Elisabeth Aigner;
Translation: Angelika Altmann-Duschlbauer, Heather Pichler;
Copy editing: Anne Schubert, Phillip Corbett (Thank you very much for your help!);
Layout and letters: Harry Friedl
ISBN 978-3-8334-8452-0

Lightning Source UK Ltd.
Milton Keynes UK
UKOW041808110912

198858UK00001B/31/A